'With great clarity and originality, Kyle Johannsen redirects our view of current discussions about social justice. By asking us to consider substantive debates as based on conceptual disagreements, he opens up new paths for philosophical research in a highly productive and inspiring way.'

—*Rainer Forst, Professor of Political Theory and Philosophy, Goethe University Frankfurt*

'A fascinating book showing how disagreement about what justice requires often reflects confusion or disagreement about the very concept of 'justice'. More controversially, it argues, with great clarity and rigor, that there is a particular way in which the concept of justice should be understood and used.'

—*Patrick Tomlin, Associate Professor in Political Philosophy, University of Reading*

A Conceptual Investigation of Justice

Conceptual analysis has fallen out of favor in political philosophy. The influence of figures like John Rawls and Ronald Dworkin has led political philosophy to focus on questions about what should be done, and to ignore questions about the usage of words.

In this book, Kyle Johannsen calls for renewed attention to the manner in which the word 'justice' is and should be used. Focusing on the late work of G. A. Cohen, Johannsen argues that debates over both the content and scope of egalitarian justice are, to a large extent, really just conceptual. Whereas some philosophers have been using the term 'justice' to refer to one among a plurality of values, others have been using it to refer to institutional rightness. Though the latter use of 'justice' is presently more dominant, he argues that much is to be gained from thinking of justice as one value among many. Doing so sheds light on the nature of both democracy and legitimacy, and, paradoxically, makes better sense of the idea that justice is 'the first virtue of institutions.'

Kyle Johannsen is Visiting Assistant Professor in the Philosophy Department at Trent University, Canada. He is primarily interested in political philosophy, meta-ethical issues that pertain to political philosophy, and animal ethics. His work has appeared in such journals as *Ethical Theory and Moral Practice*, *Res Publica*, *Ethical Perspectives*, and *Socialist Studies*.

Routledge Innovations in Political Theory

For a full list of titles in this series, please visit www.routledge.com

66 **Hegel, Marx, and 21st Century Social Movements**
Democracy, Dialectics, and Difference
Brian Lovato

67 **Ideologies of Experience**
Trauma, Failure, and the Abandonment of the Self
Matthew H. Bowker

68 **Post-Politics in Context**
Ali Rıza Taşkale

69 **Claus Offe and the Critical Theory of the Capitalist State**
Jens Borchert and Stephan Lessenich

70 **Equality Renewed**
Christine Sypnowich

71 **Rethinking Utopia: Place, Power, Affect**
David M. Bell

72 **Hugo Grotius and the Modern Theology of Freedom**
Jeremy Seth Geddert

73 **Critical Urban Theory, Common Property, and "the Political"**
Desire and Drive in the City
Dan Webb, PhD

74 **Democracy Beyond the Nation State**
Practicing Equality
Joe Parker

75 **A Conceptual Investigation of Justice**
Kyle Johannsen

A Conceptual Investigation of Justice

Kyle Johannsen

Routledge
Taylor & Francis Group
LONDON AND NEW YORK

First published 2018 by Routledge

2 Park Square, Milton Park, Abingdon, Oxfordshire OX14 4RN
52 Vanderbilt Avenue, New York, NY 10017

Routledge is an imprint of the Taylor & Francis Group, an informa business

First issued in paperback 2019

Library of Congress Cataloging-in-Publication Data
A catalog record for this book has been requested

ISBN: 978-1-138-73600-9 (hbk)
ISBN: 978-0-367-37206-4 (pbk)

Typeset in Times New Roman
by Apex CoVantage, LLC

Contents

Acknowledgments

This book is a substantially revised version of my doctoral dissertation *On the Conceptual Status of Justice*. As such, I would like to thank my former supervisor, Christine Sypnowich, and those who were on my supervisory committee, Will Kymlicka and Alistair Macleod. Both Christine and Alistair have been involved with my work since I first began it, including the embryonic work I wrote in their graduate courses during my first year in the Ph.D. program. It is unlikely that I would have taken up this project in the first place had it not been for the excellent experience I had in their courses or for the guidance (and relative freedom) I was granted when deciding what to read and write in my second year. I'm also grateful to have had the benefit of their insights in less official contexts as well. The comments Alistair made at many of my conference presentations, and the comments Christine made at meetings of the 'Justice League,' were invaluable (as were the comments of the other members of the league!).

Will's influence on my work has also been very significant. The problems he raised helped me to determine which objections to respond to as well as to frame some of the issues I address. The arguments in this book would not be nearly as persuasive had I not been exposed to his healthy skepticism.

In addition, I would like to thank Andrew Lister and Adam Swift for serving as my external examiners and for their insightful questions and comments.

Since my graduation, Christine and Will have continued to provide me with feedback and advice. I'm grateful to Christine for encouraging me to publish my work as a monograph, and I'm grateful to both her and Will for their feedback on a draft of my book proposal. I also owe thanks to Kevin Anderson, Phil Shadd, and Jennifer Tunnicliffe for giving me access to their own, successful book proposals. Having some samples to look over was helpful.

Much of the work included in this book was presented at conferences, including those hosted by the Canadian Philosophical Association, the Canadian Section of the International Association for Philosophy of Law and Social Philosophy (as well as the parent organization itself), the North American Society for Social Philosophy, and the Association for Political Theory. I am thankful to my audiences for their comments.

Chapter 4 is largely made up of my 2016 article "Cohen's Equivocal Attack on Rawls's Basic Structure Restriction," *Ethical Perspectives* 23 (3): 499–525. I'm grateful to Peeters Publishers for granting me permission to reproduce it here.

I would also like to thank former and present graduate students in Queen's Department of Philosophy for many rewarding discussions. My interactions with them at the graduate student colloquium series, informally around the department, and over drinks at the bar have undoubtedly shaped much of my work.

Special thanks to my editor, Natalja Mortensen, for her faith in and support for my project; to Lisa Bintrim, Maria Landschoot, and Lisa Salonen, for their assistance with processing and preparing my manuscript; and to two anonymous reviewers at Routledge.

Special thanks as well to my partner, Melissa Teodoro, and to my parents, Ellen and Ross Johannsen. Their support is much appreciated.

Finally, I acknowledge financial support from Queen's University; Saint Mary's University; the Ontario Ministry of Training, Colleges, and Universities; and the Social Sciences and Humanities Research Council of Canada. Receiving financial assistance from these sources at various stages of completion made my project possible.

1 Introduction

In contemporary debates about justice, political philosophers take themselves to be engaged with a subject related to but distinct from moral rightness. Though they acknowledge that justice is a normative topic, its subject matter is generally thought to be narrower than the general nature of right and wrong. This distinction has its origins in ancient philosophy. In *The Nicomachean Ethics*, Aristotle begins his discussion of justice by distinguishing between two different but related senses of the term: a narrow sense of the word 'justice' that refers to a part of morality, specifically the part pertaining to fairness, and which bears on matters of distribution and rectification; and a broader sense of the word 'justice' that refers to moral rightness in general.[1] My book argues that a disagreement over the sense in which justice is narrower than moral rightness implicitly lies at the heart of much debate between contemporary egalitarians. On one side of the disagreement is a view shared by many contemporary liberals, most notably John Rawls, which understands narrowness in terms of context specificity. In their view, justice is specifically about the moral rightness of institutions. Put another way, they think of it as the output of practical reasoning about how institutions ought to be designed.[2] By contrast, many value pluralists, most notably Isaiah Berlin, understand justice's narrowness as singularity against a plural background. In their view, justice is one fundamental value among a plurality of fundamental values.[3] When justice is understood as one fundamental value among many, to say that something is a requirement of justice is not to say that it is required, all things considered, as the demands of justice are often not entirely feasible and must sometimes give way to the demands of competing values. Thinking of justice this way means thinking of it as an *input* in practical reasoning, rather than the *output* of it.[4] Though Berlin is probably the most prominent twentieth-century philosopher to propound the pluralist view, the most systematic and rigorous articulation of it can be found in the later work of G. A. Cohen, especially in his recent book, *Rescuing Justice and Equality*.[5] For this reason I often focus on Cohen's work especially.

My book has two main purposes. The first is to establish that the disagreement between pluralist and contextualist understandings of narrowness is theoretically significant, and the second is to establish that the pluralist understanding is the correct one. With respect to the first purpose, I'll argue that much depends on whether one understands justice in the pluralist manner or in the contextualist manner. In particular, I'll connect the question of narrowness to two prominent debates in contemporary political philosophy: the debate over the luck egalitarian theory of distributive justice, and the debate over whether distributive justice imposes requirements on the choices citizens make in their personal lives. In my view, the correct answer in each of these debates depends on how justice's narrowness should be understood.

Much contemporary debate over the content of distributive justice revolves around the theory Elizabeth Anderson dubbed 'luck egalitarianism.'[6] Luck egalitarianism, broadly speaking, is the view that inequalities traceable to choice are just, while those traceable to a person's circumstances are not. Its proponents maintain that justice supports compensating a less well-off individual insofar as her disadvantaged status is no fault of her own.[7] Since its inception in the 1980s, luck egalitarianism's coherence with certain core intuitive judgments long made it the dominant egalitarian alternative to John Rawls's theory of justice. On the one hand, the idea that inequalities traceable to circumstance are unjust explains why it seems unfair for one's endowment of natural talents or for the socio-economic class into which one is born to determine one's life prospects. It also explains what seems unfair about disabilities attributable to sheer misfortune. On the other hand, the idea that inequalities traceable to choice are just explains why it seems fair for those who gamble away their holdings or choose leisure over work to have less than others.[8] In recent years, however, critics of luck egalitarianism have argued that it suffers from a number of serious deficiencies. They claim, for example, that it makes extravagant metaphysical assumptions about the nature of free will,[9] expresses a disrespectful attitude towards those it would seek to assist,[10] and has counterintuitive implications.[11] What's more, critics argue that luck egalitarians misunderstand the relationship between distributive justice and the justice of a society. They maintain that egalitarian social relations are what constitute a just society, and that distributive justice is only valuable insofar as it instrumentally contributes to the realization of social equality. In their view, any plausible account of the *content* of distributive justice must be justified in light of its instrumental relationship with social equality.[12]

A second dispute also rages among contemporary egalitarians, this time concerning the *scope* of distributive justice. The central question is whether the principles of justice applicable to institutional structures are also applicable to the personal choices citizens make within those structures. According to John Rawls, for example, a society's institutions should be designed to benefit its worst-off citizens, but better-off citizens are not required to attend to worse-off citizens when making choices about employment, how to treat family members, and so on.[13] However, critics argue that a truly just society requires more than institutional justice. It requires a social ethos that motivates citizens to act upon principles of justice in their daily lives.[14] They note, among other things, that the choices which constitute informal institutions, such as the family, have a profound impact on the distribution of life prospects (just think of how unequal the distribution of benefits and burdens is within the households of certain families and the effect this has on those born into them).[15] In reply, supporters of the Rawlsian view have argued that requiring citizens to devote their everyday lives to benefitting the worst off is too demanding.[16]

In this book, I argue that proper attention to an implicit disagreement over justice's narrowness sheds light on both the dispute over luck egalitarianism and the dispute over whether institutional justice extends to the realm of personal choice. For both disputes, I claim that the correct answer depends on what one means by the term 'justice.' On the one hand, I argue that if we understand justice's narrowness in the manner Cohen and other pluralists do, that is, a conception of justice to be a conception of one fundamental value among many, then luck egalitarianism is a compelling theory. What's more, I argue that identifying justice as one fundamental value among many entails its application to the context of personal choice. On the other hand, I argue that if we understand justice's narrowness in a contextual manner, that is, understand justice to be the part of morality that pertains to how we ought to design a society's institutions, all things considered, then luck egalitarianism proves inadequate. What's more, if justice is composed of all-things-considered principles adopted for the institutional context, then it proves implausible to claim that those principles are also suitable for the personal context. If I am right about the significance of the disagreement over narrowness, then a considerable amount of dispute among contemporary egalitarians is really just conceptual. Since disputants are either unaware that they are using the term 'justice' differently, or, as with Cohen, are generally aware of it but inadvertently equivocate when responding to critics,[17] the result is that they frequently talk past each other. What's actually a disagreement over the conceptual identity of justice ends up manifesting as a dispute over content and scope.

Establishing that the disputes over content and scope are traceable to different uses of the term 'justice' does not by itself establish a philosophical issue, however. After all, there are many words in the English language that have multiple meanings. Though this sometimes makes it necessary to disambiguate how a term is being used, there's nothing wrong with sometimes using the word one way and sometimes using it another way, and thus nothing wrong with claiming that *each* use is correct. To dispel the worry that there's no philosophical issue at stake between egalitarian disputants, I argue that the disagreement between pluralists and contextualists is more than a disagreement over the sense in which justice is a part of morality. Were this the only difference between them, then it would be easy to conclude that pluralists are talking about narrow justice (fairness) and contextualists are interested in what broad justice (moral rightness) has to say about politics. In other words, it would be easy to conclude that the difference between these camps is strictly verbal. Against the 'merely verbal' interpretation, I argue that different uses of the term 'justice' reflect a theoretical disagreement. They reflect a disagreement over the manner in which fairness should be understood. On the one hand, proponents of the pluralist view think of fairness as a substantive value that must be traded off against other values when justifying action-guiding principles. In their view, substantive fairness simply *is* narrow justice and plausible action-guiding principles necessarily fall somewhat short of it, since they must reflect other values, too (see endnote18 for some qualifying remarks).[18] Proponents of the contextualist view, on the other hand, think of fairness as a procedural concept. Since the weights we assign different values are a matter about which there is reasonable disagreement, assigning weights in a fair manner ostensibly requires a kind of fairness that is not itself a value to be weighed. What is needed is a procedural concept that can justify the adopted set of weights, and the action-guiding principles that reflect those weights, to those who will be subject to the state's coercive force.[19] When fairness is understood this way, action-guiding principles are fully fair, so long as they are adopted through a fair procedure.[20] Understanding fairness procedurally, instead of substantively, therefore makes it conceptually plausible to identify narrow justice with our action-guiding institutional principles.

In response to the contextualist position, I argue that although procedural fairness is important, substantive fairness cannot be eliminated. Non-arbitrarily specifying the content of procedural fairness, whether it is the sort of procedural fairness at play in contractualist theories of justice or the sort of fairness at play in democratic procedures, requires a substantive criterion of fairness. If I am right, then narrow justice, understood in the manner pluralists do, is integral to procedural fairness and, therefore, to the legitimate use of coercion as well.

By identifying the real issue at stake in egalitarian debates over distributive justice's content and scope, this book promises to help us better understand contemporary disagreement between egalitarians. It also promises to shed light on where focusing our theoretical efforts is most likely to secure a resolution. Though I myself will argue in favor of the view that justice, properly speaking, is one fundamental value among many, it is my hope that an appreciation for the theoretical significance of the question 'What is the conceptual identity of justice?' will motivate future work that confirms, expands upon, or even contradicts my view. Only when more work has been done to answer this question will we have a clear sense of what the plausible answers are or of the reasons for and against them.

Notes

1. Aristotle (1998) Book V, Sections 1–2.
2. Rawls (1971) pp. 7–8 and 108–17; and Rawls (2001) p. 14. The claim that justice is the part of moral rightness concerned with institutions is sometimes understood in terms of 'enforceability.' On this view, duties of justice are specifically those moral duties that can legitimately be enforced by law. Of course, the state does more than just coerce people. It also, for example, provides non-coercive incentives and disincentives via tax policy and the like. The claim that the distinguishing feature

of duties of justice is their enforceability thus entails the claim that duties of justice are institutional, but the claim that they're institutional does not entail that duties of justice are limited to that which is enforceable. For examples of prominent liberal philosophers (other than Rawls) who endorse either the institutional understanding or its narrower 'enforceability' counter-part, see Kymlicka (2002) pp. 5–6; Miller (2007) pp. 248–9; Nozick (1974) p. 6; and Tan (2004b) pp. 21–9.

3. Berlin (2002). See also Feinberg (1989) pp. 108–16.
4. I borrow the terms 'input' and 'output' from Patrick Tomlin. See Tomlin (2010) p. 232.
5. Cohen (2008). For a brief statement of the view, see pp. 2–6. For his full, systematic articulation, see Chapters 6 and 7.
6. See Anderson (1999).
7. The authors in the literature don't always use this exact language, but it is generally not far off. According to Dworkin, "On the one hand, we must, on pain of violating equality, allow the distribution of resources at any particular time to be (as we might say) ambition-sensitive . . . But on the other hand, we must not allow the distribution of resources at any moment to be endowment-sensitive . . ." See Dworkin (2000) p. 89. Similarly, Richard Arneson said of his own position, "When persons enjoy equal opportunity for welfare . . . any actual inequality of welfare in the positions they reach is due to factors that lie within each individual's control." See Arneson (1989) p. 86. Likewise G. A. Cohen describes the thrust of his position as aiming ". . . to eliminate *involuntary disadvantage*, by which I (stipulatively) mean disadvantage for which the sufferer cannot be held responsible, since it does not appropriately reflect choices that he has made or is making or would make." See Cohen (1989) p. 916.
8. See Kymlicka (2002) pp. 75–9; and Kymlicka (2006) pp. 17–8.
9. See Scheffler (2003) pp. 17–9; and Scheffler (2005) pp. 10–4.
10. See Wolff (1998) pp. 110–5; and Anderson (1999) pp. 304–7.
11. See Anderson (1999) pp. 295–300; Scheffler (2003) pp. 32–3; and Scheffler (2005) pp. 15–6.
12. See Anderson (1999) pp. 312–5; Scheffler (2003) pp. 21–4 and pp. 31–9; and Scheffler (2005) pp. 17–23.
13. Rawls (1971) pp. 7–8 and pp. 108–17.
14. Cohen (1997) pp. 3–30; Murphy (1999) pp. 251–91.
15. Cohen (2008) pp. 136–7.
16. For an articulation of the demandingness critique, see Pogge (2000) pp. 152–4 and pp. 163–4. For other discussions of this worry, see Van Parijs (1993); Tan (2004a); and Titelbaum (2008).
17. I make this criticism of Cohen in Chapter 4.
18. That fairness and narrow justice are the same thing seems to be Cohen's view throughout much of his work. In one of his last papers, however, he adopts the view that substantive fairness is a part of, rather than the whole of, justice (though he still maintains that most values are external to justice), and a number of like-minded theorists hold that view as well. My own view, however, is that compromising justice's association with fairness is conceptually problematic, and I argue for that claim in Chapter 5. For expressions of the view that substantive fairness is merely a part of justice, see, for example, Segall (2007) p. 188; Swift (2008) pp. 382–3; Tomlin (2010) p. 244; and Cohen (2011) pp. 124–43. See also Cohen's non-committal comments in Cohen (2009) p. 37.
19. See Rawls's discussion of weights and the priority problem in Rawls (1971) pp. 34–45. For a discussion of contractualist justification as justification *to* citizens, that is, as interpersonal justification, see Anderson (2010) pp. 1–23.
20. Rawls (2001) p. 16.

References

Anderson, Elizabeth. 1999. "What Is the Point of Equality?" *Ethics* 109: 287–337.

Anderson, Elizabeth. 2010. "The Fundamental Disagreement between Luck Egalitarians and Relational Egalitarians." *Canadian Journal of Philosophy* 40(suppl. 1): 1–23.

Aristotle. 1998. *Aristotle: The Nicomachean Ethics*. Trans. W. D. Ross (Oxford: Oxford University Press).

Arneson, Richard. 1989. "Equality and Equal Opportunity for Welfare." *Philosophical Studies* 56: 77–93.

Berlin, Isaiah. 2002. "Two Concepts of Liberty." In *Liberty: Incorporating Four Essays on Liberty*. Ed. Henry Hardy (Oxford: Oxford University Press).

Cohen, G. A. 1989. "On the Currency of Egalitarian Justice." *Ethics* 99: 906–44.

Cohen, G. A. 1997. "Where the Action Is: On the Site of Distributive Justice." *Philosophy and Public Affairs* 26: 3–30.

Cohen, G. A. 2008. *Rescuing Justice and Equality* (Cambridge, MA: Harvard University Press).

Cohen, G. A. 2009. *Why Not Socialism?* (Princeton, NJ: Princeton University Press).

Cohen, G. A. 2011. "Fairness and Legitimacy in Justice, and: Does Option Luck Ever Preserve Justice?" In *On the Currency of Egalitarian Justice, and Other Essays in Political Philosophy*. Ed. Michael Otsuka (Princeton: Princeton University Press). Pp. 124–43.

Dworkin, Ronald. 2000. *Sovereign Virtue*: *The Theory and Practice of Equality* (Cambridge, MA: Harvard University Press).

Feinberg, Joel. 1989. "Rawls and Intuitionism." In *Reading Rawls: Critical Studies on Rawls' 'A Theory of Justice'*. Ed. Norman Daniels (Stanford: Stanford University Press). Pp. 108–24.

Kymlicka, Will. 2002. *Contemporary Political Philosophy: An Introduction* (New York: Oxford University Press).

Kymlicka, Will. 2006. "Left-Liberalism Revisited." In *The Egalitarian Conscience: Essays in Honor of G.A. Cohen*. Ed. Christine Sypnowich (New York: Oxford University Press). Pp. 9–35.

Miller, David. 2007. *National Responsibility and Global Justice* (Oxford: Oxford University Press).

Murphy, Liam B. 1999. "Institutions and the Demands of Justice." *Philosophy and Public Affairs* 27: 251–91.

Nozick, Robert. 1974. *Anarchy, State, and Utopia* (New York: Basic Books).

Pogge, Thomas. 2000. "On the Site of Distributive Justice: Reflections on Cohen and Murphy." *Philosophy and Public Affairs* 29: 137–69.

Rawls, John. 1971. *A Theory of Justice* (Cambridge, MA: Belknap Press).

Rawls, John. 2001. *Justice as Fairness: A Restatement*. Ed. Erin Kelly (Cambridge, MA: Belknap Press).

Scheffler, Samuel. 2003. "What Is Egalitarianism?" *Philosophy and Public Affairs* 31: 5–39.

Scheffler, Samuel. 2005. "Choice, Circumstance, and the Value of Equality." *Politics, Philosophy, and Economics* 4: 5–28.

Segall, Shlomi. 2007. "In Solidarity with the Imprudent: A Defense of Luck Egalitarianism." *Social Theory and Practice* 33: 177–98.

Swift, Adam. 2008. "The Value of Philosophy in Non-Ideal Circumstances." *Social Theory and Practice* 34: 363–87.

Tan, Kok-Chor. 2004a. "Justice and Personal Pursuits." *The Journal of Philosophy* 101: 331–62.

Tan, Kok-Chor. 2004b. *Justice without Borders* (Cambridge: Cambridge University Press).

Titelbaum, Michael G. 2008. "What Would a Rawlsian Ethos of Justice Look Like?" *Philosophy and Public Affairs* 36: 289–322.

Tomlin, Patrick. 2010. "Survey Article: Internal Doubts about Cohen's Rescue of Justice." *The Journal of Political Philosophy* 18: 228–47.

Van Parijs, Philippe. 1993. "Rawlsians, Christians and Patriots." *European Journal of Philosophy* 1: 309–42.

Wolff, Jonathan. 1998. "Fairness, Respect, and the Egalitarian Ethos." *Philosophy and Public Affairs* 27: 97–122.

2 Fairness, Efficiency, and Value Theory

1. Introduction

The purpose of this chapter is to set the stage for subsequent chapters. Throughout the book, I assume that fairness and efficiency are distinct and sometimes conflicting values. Since this assumption is a contestable one, I defend it here in section 2. Furthermore, an important distinction I employ throughout the book is the distinction between a principle that expresses the content of a particular value vs. an action-guiding or all-things-considered or regulatory principle (the word I use varies to some extent from chapter to chapter). Since this distinction is a key one in future chapters, I discuss it here in section 3. In particular, I argue that justifying a conception of a value is different from justifying an action-guiding principle: whereas the intuitive judgments of interest to us in the latter case are our all-things-considered judgments of right and wrong, the intuitive judgments of interest to us in the former cases are specifically those internal to the value in question. With these preliminary matters covered, the material covered in subsequent chapters will hopefully be more digestible as well as more plausible.

2. Fairness and Efficiency

This section is about two of the values with which I will be concerned at various points throughout the book: fairness and efficiency. One reason for discussing them here is that I think it will be helpful for the reader to have a sense of what I have in mind when I use these terms. Another is that I assume throughout that fairness and efficiency are values that sometimes conflict with each other, particularly in cases where the implementation of distributive equality requires levelling down. In my analysis, an analysis shared by, for example, G. A. Cohen and Larry Temkin, levelling down for the sake of achieving distributive equality, though morally problematic, is nonetheless conducive to fairness.[1] The problem with levelling down is not unfairness, on this view, but rather inefficiency. However, understanding fairness and efficiency to be values that conflict with each other is controversial for a number of reasons. For starters, it might be argued that efficiency is not a distinct value. Efficiency, according to some, is strictly an instrumental concept. If this is so, then arguably the relevant value in discussions of efficiency is whatever X or Xs we're interested in efficiently promoting.[2]

Second, it might be argued that even if efficiency is a distinct value, it nonetheless cannot come into conflict with fairness, as the presuppositions that lie behind fairness prevent this from being plausible. In one version of this objection, fairness cannot conflict with efficiency because fairness presupposes efficiency. According to the objector, fairly distributing something is only of moral significance when the thing we want to distribute is something that should be efficiently promoted.[3] In another version of this objection, fairness cannot conflict with efficiency because both are grounded in a more fundamental value, namely concern for the well-being of persons. More specifically, since levelling down is patently at odds with concern for the well-being of persons, and since fairness is parasitic upon concern, it cannot be said that fairness is ceteris paribus in favor of levelling down while efficiency is not. Whatever is parasitic upon concern cannot also conflict with concern.[4]

Before addressing these objections, two prefatory remarks are in order. First, the term 'levelling down,' as I will use it throughout the book, refers to the selection of a state of affairs in which everyone is worse off than they otherwise would be in some alternative state of affairs. The reason I mention this is because the term is sometimes used in a different way in the philosophical literature. In some cases, 'levelling down' is used to refer to the selection of an egalitarian state of affairs in which everyone is equally badly off over an alternative, unequal state of affairs in which some are better off and no one is worse off.[5] My own use of the term is not idiosyncratic, however. Much of the literature on levelling down specifically employs the 'everyone's worse off' use of it.[6] My reason for using the term this way is because it is the version of 'levelling down' relevant to discussions about economic incentives. As we will see in Chapter 4, many liberals believe that the inequalities that economic incentives create are morally necessary because doing away with incentives would leave us all worse off. Since I am mainly interested in discussing levelling down as it pertains to incentives, I will specifically be using the term in cases where a course of action would leave everyone worse off than they otherwise would be.

Second, it should be noted that the characterization of fairness I am going to offer is specifically meant to apply to substantive fairness, that is, to a substantive value that should be predicated of distributions to the extent that they satisfy the best principle of fairness. Noting this at the outset is important because there are common senses of the word 'fairness' to which my characterization of the concept is not meant to apply, a prominent example of which is procedural fairness. Much of what I will say about substantive fairness is not true of procedural fairness. For example, while I think substantive fairness can come into conflict with efficiency, I do not think that it makes any sense to say procedural fairness does so. To the contrary, as I will explain in Chapter 5, the function of procedural fairness is to help us adjudicate between conflicting values by picking out a particular set of action-guiding principles that reflect a specific balance between the values. Understood this way, fairness is not one of the values that potentially conflicts with efficiency, and it would certainly never require us to level down, even in the ceteris paribus sense of the word 'require.' The reason I take myself to be justified in claiming that fairness conflicts with efficiency is because I think a substantive understanding of fairness, one that luck egalitarianism supplies the content of (see Chapter 3, this volume, for my arguments to that effect), cannot be replaced by a procedural understanding of fairness. In fact, I think substantive fairness is needed to non-arbitrarily specify the content of an optimally fair procedure and is thus more fundamental than procedural fairness. It is not until Chapter 5 that I will justify this claim, though.

Let us begin with the first objection, namely the claim that efficiency is not a value at all. The claim that efficiency is not a value is based on the idea that considering it to be such is inconsistent with the way we use the word in every-day language. The every-day concept of 'efficiency,' as Alistair Macleod puts it, is an 'end-presupposing' rather than an 'end-incorporating' notion. In his understanding, whether an agent's course of action is efficient is always relative to the pursuit of some X, where X stands for one of the agent's goals. To say that efficiency is end-presupposing, rather than end-incorporating, is to say that the content of the X depends on the agent's goal set, rather than on the concept of efficiency itself. As a result, we cannot know in advance of asking the agent what end it is that she is interested in efficiently pursuing. According to Macleod, it is appropriate to predicate efficiency of a course of action when that action effectively and economically achieves the end at which it aims, and when it does so in a manner that is broadly consistent with the agent's other ends.[7]

Aside from a minor reservation about Macleod's 'other ends' constraint on judgments of efficiency,[8] I think his account does an excellent job of capturing the every-day concept of efficiency. What's more, I also think he is right to say that the every-day concept of efficiency is not a distinct value. After all, the every-day concept can be attached to just about any goal, including the pursuit of things that arguably *are* distinct values, such as the pursuit of fairness, community, and so on. Thus, I agree that the X to which every-day efficiency attaches, rather than efficiency itself, is the relevant value when efficiency language is used in discussions about justice and morality.

Where I disagree is with the claim that those who do think of 'efficiency' as a value have the every-day concept of it in mind when they use that word. In Macleod's view, proponents of, for example, the Pareto understanding of efficiency are importantly wrong because they're allegedly aiming at but failing to capture the every-day concept.[9] As far as I can tell, though, this is not the case. Instead, the Pareto conception of efficiency is aiming at a different concept, one that bears some resemblance to but nonetheless differs from the every-day one. Let's call this second concept of 'efficiency' the quantitative concept.[10]

What is the quantitative concept of efficiency? Characterizing it without presupposing any particular conception is a bit tricky, but I think it suffices to say that it pertains to increasing the amount of a quantifiable good.[11] It is this quantitative sense of the word 'efficiency' that, for example, Rawls employs when he claims that both a principle that mandates maximizing the aggregate amount and a principle that mandates the achievement of Pareto-optimality are appropriately dubbed 'principles of efficiency.'[12] The main way in which different conceptions of quantitative efficiency differently interpret the concept is with respect to the words 'increasing' and 'amount.' With respect to 'amount,' at least two interpretations immediately present themselves: 'aggregate amount' and 'average amount.' The second of these is, for example, employed by the version of utilitarianism Rawls wrestles with in his efforts to show that his two principles are comparatively superior for regulating the basic structure of society.[13] With respect to the word 'increasing,' two interpretations also present themselves more or less immediately. The first interprets the word in the strongest sense possible; that is, 'increasing' is understood to mean 'maximizing.' The second, in contrast, interprets the word in a more qualified fashion. In this interpretation, the word is understood to mean 'increasing so long as no particular person incurs a loss.' This second way of interpreting 'increasing' is the sense employed by the Pareto-optimality version of efficiency that Rawls claims hypothetical contractors in the original position would adopt to evaluate the efficiency of institutional arrangements.[14]

With respect to the goods to which the quantitative sense of efficiency might be applied, some are more easily analyzed as quantities of discrete units than others. Subjective welfare and flourishing, for example, perhaps defy being cardinally represented through the use of numbers. So long as we can intelligibly discuss these concepts via the use of quantity presupposing ordinal language, though—for example, can intelligibly talk about differing 'levels' of flourishing or welfare, or about some people having 'more' or 'less' flourishing or welfare—then the concept of efficiency applies.

As I have described it, the concept of efficiency is largely, though not entirely, indeterminate. There's the indeterminacy I have mentioned with respect to the terms 'increasing' and 'amount.' There is also indeterminacy with respect to the quantifiable good to which this concept might be applied; for example, we might speak of efficiency with respect to welfare or with respect to primary goods. As such, it would be fine for a person with a maximum aggregate conception of efficiency to substitute talk about maximizing resources for talk about efficiently promoting them. Unlike the every-day concept of efficiency, however, there is not enough indeterminacy within the quantitative concept for it to be applied to any X. For example, while it would be fine for someone employing the every-day sense of the term 'efficiency' to speak of efficiently pursuing a fair distribution of resources, it would not be fine for someone employing the quantitative concept to do so. Regardless of what one's conception of the quantitative concept might be, so long as the concept behind the term 'efficiency' is understood to pertain to increasing the amount of a quantifiable good, then it makes no sense to speak of efficiently promoting a fair distribution of resources, nor, for that matter, of efficiency with respect to the promotion of anything that is not a quantifiable good.

Of course, the quantitative concept can be appropriately applied in a secondary manner to non-goods, such as societies. A society that efficiently promotes the goods over which it exerts influence is appropriately described as efficient. In this same sense, were it the case, hypothetically speaking, that pursuing a fair distribution of a good is conducive to increasing the amount of that good, then it would make sense to say that the pursuit of fairness is efficient. It is to quantifiable goods, however, that the quantitative sense of the term 'efficient' primarily applies. Any application of the quantitative sense to societies or other subjects is only appropriate when those subjects are themselves efficient promoters of goods.

It might be objected that the distinction I have drawn between the quantitative and every-day concepts of efficiency does not suffice to justify the claim that there is a sense of the word 'efficiency' that refers to a value. According to my objector, the quantitative concept of efficiency is just as instrumental as the every-day concept. The only difference is that the range of Xs to which the former might be applied is more restricted than the range of Xs to which the latter might be applied. If this is so, then just as with the every-day concept of efficiency, it is allegedly incorrect to claim that the quantitative concept, rather than the X to which it is applied, is the relevant value. The values of interest when using the quantitative concept in normative deliberation are things like welfare, resources, flourishing, and so forth.[15]

While I agree that there's a sense in which the quantitative concept of efficiency is instrumental, I do not think it is correct to say that efficiency therefore is not a distinct value. Efficiency certainly presupposes the importance of what it applies to. Why, for example, would we want *more* flourishing unless flourishing were something of value? However, to say that the value of efficiency *presupposes* the value of the X to which it applies is not the same thing as saying that it can be *replaced* by that X. The claim that flourishing is valuable is much vaguer than the claim that more flourishing is better, ceteris paribus, than less flourishing. Unlike the bald claim that flourishing is valuable, the claim that more flourishing is better, ceteris paribus, than less flourishing, tells us what we have reason to pursue given that flourishing is valuable, specifically that we have reason to pursue more of it.

That presupposing the value of an X is different from being replaceable by that X can be further demonstrated by noting that the importance of fairly distributing an X presupposes its value just as much as the importance of pursuing a larger quantity of it. As with efficiency, it does not make any sense to care about fairly distributing a quantifiable good unless that good is valuable. But that does not mean fairness isn't a value. The claim that we have a defeasible reason to pursue a fair distribution of some X is more specific than the claim that X is valuable. It tells us what we have reason to pursue given the value of the X, specifically that we have reason to care that it be distributed in a fair manner.[16]

This is probably a good place to discuss the concept I have in mind when I use the term 'fairness.' Following Jeremy Waldron, I think it is accurate to say that fairness is about "distributive information across individuals."[17] Or, if that is a bit too obscure, that fairness is about who has what and why. To better see what Waldron and I mean, it is helpful to contrast the concept of fairness with the concept of efficiency.[18] As we noted earlier, efficiency is about increasing the amount of a good. If we want to compare the efficiency of two distributions, then all we need to refer to is the relevant amount in each. If we are specifically interested in Pareto-optimality, then, assuming no individual in either distribution incurred a loss, the distribution with the highest amount should be considered the most efficient one. If we are specifically interested in maximizing the average amount, then the distribution with the highest average should be deemed the most efficient. Either way, the kind of information we're interested in when comparing distributions from the standpoint of efficiency is entirely impersonal. We do not need to know any information about the individual shareholders.

By contrast, suppose we are interested in comparing the extent to which two distributions are egalitarian. In order to make this comparison, information about individual shareholders is essential. More specifically, we need to know the number of shareholders in each distribution and the size of each individual's share before we can accurately calculate the extent to which either distribution is an equal one. Similarly, if we were interested in comparing the extent to which, say, two distributions allocate shares in accordance with considerations of desert or personal merit, then information about individual shareholders would again be essential. We would want to know the number of shares and the size of each, as well as the deservingness of each individual. In both cases, information about individual shareholders is essential to comparing the distributions; thus, both equality and desert can appropriately be considered conceptions of fairness.

Though I hope to have established that the objections I have addressed fail to undermine the claim that efficiency is a value, there are other objections that accept efficiency as a value and yet reject the possibility that it conflicts with fairness. According to Thomas Christiano, fairness presupposes efficiency, and thus fairness cannot give us even a defeasible reason to level down. He points out that in all cases where it is reasonable to care about whether a good is fairly distributed (he specifically has egalitarian distribution in mind), it is also true that more of that good is to be preferred over less of that good. Were it not the case that more of a particular good is to be preferred over less of it, the good's distribution would be morally irrelevant. From this, Christiano infers that fairness cannot require levelling down. Since fairness is parasitic upon efficiency, it can only give us a reason to prefer the more egalitarian state of affairs among a set of equally efficient states of affairs. It cannot give us a reason to prefer the more egalitarian state of affairs among a set that includes less egalitarian but more efficient states of affairs.[19]

The mistake in Christiano's line of reasoning is analogous to what is referred to as the 'common cause fallacy.' The common cause fallacy is committed when someone thinks X causes Y because X and Y always coincide and fails to observe that Z is the cause of both. In Christiano's case, the analogous mistake is thinking that the importance of fairly distributing a good is parasitic upon the importance of efficiently promoting it because the two always coincide and thereby failing to notice that it is simply the value of the good that accounts for why both fair distribution and efficient promotion matter. I have already devoted some space to discussing the idea that the fair distribution and efficient promotion of a good presuppose but are more specific than the notion that the good is valuable. I will not go on about it at too much length here, but I will say that we have good reason to think that fairness and efficiency apply because of a good's value, rather than that fairness applies to a good because efficiency applies to that good too. It is hard to make sense of why we have reason to prefer the fairer of two equally efficient distributions if fairness is parasitic upon efficiency. On the assumption that there is no difference between the efficiency of two distributions, efficiency, as well as anything parasitic upon it, is presumably indifferent between them. In contrast, if we understand both fairness and efficiency as parasitic upon the *value* of a good, then we have an explanation readily available. The fairer of two equally efficient distributions of a good is to be preferred because efficiency does not exhaust what is required in light of that good's value. In addition to implying that more is better than less, the value of a quantifiable good also implies that we have a defeasible reason to fairly distribute it.

The last objection states that fairness and efficiency do not conflict because both are derived from a more fundamental value, namely concern for the well-being of persons, and levelling down is inconsistent with concern. The general thought here is similar to Christiano's. If making everyone worse off is inconsistent with concern for their well-being, and fairness is derivable from concern, then fairness cannot give us a reason to level down. A subordinate value cannot give us a reason to do something that the more fundamental value it's derived from condemns.[20]

In Chapter 5, I will discuss the concept of concern as it appears in Dworkin's idea of abstract equality, that is, the idea of equal concern for the fate of citizens.[21] Since I will be discussing abstract equality at length there, I do not want to say too much about it here. What I will say, however, is that on my analysis, concern is best understood as a particularly compelling conception of efficiency, rather than as a separable fundamental value that underlies both fairness and efficiency. Understanding efficiency as specifically about increasing 'the good' of people, rather than increasing the amount of 'the good' in general, avoids the counter-intuitive implication that an efficient society is one that sacrifices existing people's good for the sake of increasing the total amount of 'the good' through population growth.[22] Thus, while I agree that levelling down is inconsistent with concern for the well-being of persons, I do not think this shows that efficient inequalities are therefore fair. Fairness, understood as a substantive value (rather than procedurally), can conflict with concern for the well-being of persons. One case where it does so is when levelling down is needed to achieve equality. That fairness is best understood as independent of and thus not derivable from concern is bolstered by the thought that concern is something that can be exercised unfairly. A government that, for example, devotes a great deal of resources to promoting the well-being of one social group but devotes very little in the way of resources to promoting the well-being of other social groups does not fail to express concern. It simply expresses concern unfairly. If fairness were parasitic upon concern, though, then we would not be able to make sense of this judgment, nor of the related judgment that concern should be balanced against considerations of fairness. A subordinate value tells us what the more fundamental value it's derived from requires of us: it does not compete with the more fundamental value.

3. Theorizing Values

(a) Internal and External Intuitive Judgments

In the previous section, I hope to have established that it is plausible to think of fairness and efficiency as separate, sometimes competing values. Though I mentioned that various conceptions of these values are available, I did not say anything about the method one might use to adjudicate between conceptions. In this section, my goal is to layout the manner in which I think a conception of a fundamental value should be justified. Doing so will set the stage for the next chapter, where I argue that luck egalitarianism is compelling so long as it is understood as a conception of fairness.

To get a handle on what offering a conception of a fundamental value involves, it will be helpful to contrast it with a similar, though importantly different, process: reflective equilibrium. As Rawls and others characterize it, justifying action-guiding principles via reflective equilibrium involves seeking coherence between them and one's considered intuitive judgments about particular cases of right and wrong. For instance, if consistently applying one's conception of the best all-things-considered principles of institutional design requires prescribing slavery in our present circumstances, then that conception is out of sync with an important moral judgment. Faced with this inconsistency, the theorist has two options. The first is to revise her conception in order to render it consistent with the judgment that slavery is wrong. Doing so is the best choice available when it can be done without running afoul of other important judgments. Alternatively, she can discard the inconsistent judgment, thereby leaving her original principles unmodified. This, however, should only be done if modification would be too costly.[23]

The above characterization of reflective equilibrium leaves out many of the relevant theoretical complexities, such as the filtration process an intuitive judgment must pass through in order to qualify as 'considered' and the distinction between 'wide' and 'narrow' reflective equilibrium.[24] However, for our purposes we can leave such complexities aside and focus on the main feature with respect to which reflective equilibrium, generally conceived, differs from the method in question, namely the status of the intuitions one hopes to attain coherence with. With reflective equilibrium, the intuitions one is interested in achieving coherence with are those about what, all things considered, is right or wrong to do in particular situations we could plausibly find ourselves in. Such intuitions are important to take account of when adopting action-guiding principles, for a principle that runs afoul of them will ostensibly fail to provide morally adequate guidance in at least some cases. In contrast, the intuitions of interest when offering a conception of a fundamental value are, on the one hand, not restricted to those we have about situations we could plausibly find ourselves in (some intuitions of interest may be about strictly hypothetical scenarios). On the other hand, though, they are also fairly narrow. This means, in part, that they will tend not to be normatively decisive except in the ceteris paribus sense. It also means that there are many intuitive judgments that, though normatively significant, are external to the value in question and thus irrelevant to the project of articulating a conception of it.

Let us draw on a particular example. Consider the well-known conception of personal autonomy articulated by Harry Frankfurt in his piece "Freedom of the Will and the Concept of a Person."[25] According to Frankfurt, a necessary and sufficient condition for an action's autonomy is that it flows from a volition that is itself the object of a second-order volition; that is, an action is autonomous if and only if the agent, upon critical reflection, decides that she wants to want to perform it.[26] Conceiving of autonomy in this way effectively builds upon Hume's classic form of compatibilism.[27] It requires that the 'nature' (first order desires) in accordance with which one acts be endorsed by the agent herself, thereby removing much of the counter-intuitiveness associated with the idea that one is free so long as one is not prevented from acting in accordance with desires that have themselves been determined by biological and sociological forces.

Since its publication in 1971, Frankfurt's conception of personal autonomy has been subjected to a significant amount of critical attention, much of which has focused on the idea that his subjective criterion must be (a) modified and/or (b) supplemented with one or more objective criteria.[28] Without such modification and/or supplementation, the theory is unable to deal with a range of cases where the process through which one forms second-order volitions is tainted by autonomy undermining influences, such as brainwashing.

To amend a conception of autonomy in response to such cases is eminently reasonable. Brainwashing straightforwardly undermines the agent's ability to perform autonomous acts. As such, it is important to ensure that the content of one's criteria for autonomy not require deeming such cases to be compatible with autonomous action. Adding a condition that, for instance, places restrictions upon the process via which second-order volitions are formed is one way to try to avoid this problem.[29] However, there are considerations pertaining to the formation of second-order volitions that, though normatively relevant, need not be taken into account when formulating a conception of personal autonomy. For example, almost no one has an entirely optimal set of first-order desires. Some desires would, if acted upon, cause harm to oneself (and perhaps others) over either the short or long term, such as a desire to over-indulge in sweets, drink too much, and so on. From an outsider's standpoint, it seems clear that the agent ought not endorse, or subsequently act upon, desires that will predictably cause harm. However, cases where she fails to do so are not counter-examples to the claim that endorsement is necessary and sufficient for autonomy. Establishing that to endorse a desire for excessive chocolate consumption is to endorse something harmful to one's health is not to establish that the actions that flow from said desire are non-autonomous (at least not without assuming a considerable amount of philosophical artifice in the background). Instead, it draws attention to the fact that the action lacks another virtue, probably prudence. Considerations concerning which first-order desires are consistent with prudence, though normatively significant, are ostensibly external to a conception of autonomy. They should be taken into account by the agent when deciding which desires to identify with, as should considerations concerning which desires reflect other virtues, such as compassion, loyalty, and so on, but they are irrelevant to the criteria that constitute autonomous actions.

If narrow justice is indeed best understood as one fundamental value among many (a claim that I will not argue for until Chapter 5), then justifying a conception of it requires testing that conception against one's intuitive judgments, but not all judgments are relevant. Many of the intuitive judgments trotted out in opposition to, for instance, egalitarian principles of justice, are ostensibly external.[30] For example, consider the judgment that 'levelling down ought to be avoided, all things considered.' It is often thought to be a serious problem for a theory of justice if it requires us to make everyone worse off than they previously were. Though levelling down is of course to be avoided, is it to be avoided specifically because it is *unfair* for everyone to have less for the sake of equality? This is not obvious. A far more obvious explanation is that we care about efficiency, and levelling down is *guaranteed* to be inefficient. It is certainly always inefficient from the standpoint of Pareto-optimality, as any state of affairs in which there is unrealized potential for some to have more without others incurring a loss is Pareto-sub-optimal. More strikingly, levelling down is also always inefficient from the standpoint of a conception that mandates maximizing either the aggregate or average amount. Though losses for some people are consistent with increasing aggregate and average amounts in cases where those losses are offset by greater gains for other people, levelling down involves, by definition, losses to all shareholders. It is thus analytically true that levelling down is inefficient from the standpoint of all three of the above conceptions of efficiency.[31] What's more, the cost involved in levelling down is not merely an opportunity cost. Sometimes when we speak of an outcome as being inefficient, what we mean is that it is less efficient than some other possible outcome we could have achieved. For example, increasing the sum of a good by twenty units might appropriately be thought of as inefficient if we could have increased it by forty units instead (though perhaps limiting ourselves to a twenty-unit increase was preferable if it allowed us to achieve some other benefit, such as greater distributive equality). When we level down, though, the loss experienced is not an opportunity cost. Everyone has less than they originally did, so levelling down involves a pure cost.

In contrast with the judgment that 'levelling down ought to be avoided, all things considered,' there are a range of intuitive judgments that do pertain specifically to fairness and are thus relevant to discovering the content of narrow justice. As we noted earlier, fairness pertains to distributive information across individuals, that is, to who has what and why. Thus for a judgment to be appropriately deemed a judgment of fairness, its application must presuppose information about individual shareholders, such as information about the relative size of their shares, personal information about particular shareholders, and so forth. For example, the abstract judgment that 'it is unfair for the talented to have a greater share of resources on account of genetic fortune,' when applied in criticism of a particular distribution, presupposes a certain amount of information about that distribution's individual shareholders. More specifically, it presupposes the following details: (a) ordinal information about individual shares, that is, that some shareholders have more than others; (b) ordinal information about the physical and/or mental characteristics of shareholders, that is, that the individuals with larger shares have superior natural talents; and (c) information about the extent to which shareholders are responsible for their differing shares, that is, that their differing shares are in part traceable to differences of talent and that talents are largely the product of genetic luck. The judgment that it is unfair for someone to have more than others on account of natural talents is thus highly individual. By contrast, the judgment that 'levelling down ought to be avoided' is impersonal. Its application does not presuppose any information about the relative sizes of shares (Which shares are larger? By how much?), about the characteristics of shareholders (Who's the most deserving? Who has the greatest need?), or about the origins of shares (Are they traceable to genetic luck? To fully consensual transactions?). A judgment's application need not presuppose all these kinds of individualized information in order to qualify as a judgment of fairness. It must, however, presuppose some of them. If it does not, then it is not a judgment about distributive information across individuals, and thus not a judgment of fairness. Taking note of this is important. Only judgments of fairness are internal to the project of articulating a criterion necessary and sufficient for the fairness of distributions.[32]

What I have said thus far hopefully suffices to establish the plausibility of distinguishing between intuitive judgments that are internal to fairness and those that are external to fairness. Though I have mostly spoken of the distinction between efficiency and fairness thus far, I also think that we can (and do) isolate judgments that belong to other discrete values, such as autonomy. Furthermore, I think that any effort to articulate a conception of a particular fundamental value must be informed by a sense of which judgments are internal to that value. This holds true regardless of whether the value one seeks to theorize is fairness, personal autonomy, efficiency, and so on.

(b) Are Internality and Externality Post-Theoretical?

At this point, it might be objected that whether a judgment is internal or external to a value depends on one's conception of that value. According to my objector, it is not possible to pre-theoretically determine what does or does not belong to a value. Such a distinction putatively presupposes knowledge of the value's content, and if we know the value's content, then we already have a conception of it in mind when we claim that a judgment is consistent or inconsistent with it. Consider once more my claim that considerations of efficiency are external to fairness. Might there be a conception of fairness under which fairness and efficiency coincide with each other? There is, in fact, such a conception. A number of theorists have noted that it is possible to interpret utilitarianism as a conception of fairness. How so? Fairness yields the maximization of subjective welfare when we understand fairness to be a matter of giving equal weight to the welfare of every shareholder.[33] When fairness is understood to require equally weighing the promotion of each shareholder's welfare, the result is that achieving a fair distribution becomes a matter of achieving an efficient one. On a utilitarian understanding of fairness, anytime there is a choice to be made about distributing a unit of some good, such as income, fairness will always require that the unit in question be given to the person who will derive the most utility from it. To do otherwise would require according the promotion of that person's utility less weight then the promotion of others' utility and is thus tantamount, on the utilitarian conception of fairness, to treating that person unfairly. Our objector maintains that when fairness is understood in a utilitarian manner, it is then incorrect to insist upon a rigid distinction between considerations of fairness, on the one hand, and considerations of efficiency, on the other. In the utilitarian view, fairness and efficiency go hand in hand.

I have two points to make in reply to the above objection. First, using a conception of fairness to determine what counts as a judgment of fairness puts the cart before the horse. It is methodologically unsound to say that "seemingly unfair situations X, Y, and Z actually aren't unfair because my theory says so."[34] A pre-theoretical sense of what is or is not internal to fairness, of what is or is not internal to autonomy, and so on, is necessary before one can go about theorizing the relevant value, and if a particular conception of a value runs afoul of a relevant pre-theoretical judgments, then so much the worse for that theory. Of course, if the theory is in all other respects a compelling one, then we might decide to treat the judgments that conflict with it as outlier judgments that should be put aside (though not forgotten about) for the sake of a principle that successfully coheres with most other relevant judgments. However, to maintain that our pre-theoretical judgments of fairness are not really judgments of fairness unless supported by our chosen principle of fairness is to deprive us of the materials needed to fashion a justified conception of fairness in the first place. After all, if the pedigree of our judgments of fairness depended upon our theory of fairness, then they could not be invoked in support of our theory of fairness.

Whatever prima facie plausibility my objector's objection has is, I think, traceable to a failure to appreciate how useful value *concepts* can be. Though my objector is right to say that we need to know something about a value before we can say which judgments belong to it, we do not need to have anything like a worked out *conception* of it in advance. It suffices to have a general sense of what that value is about. Of course, it is always possible for a dispute to emerge over whether or not a judgment is internal. The reason such dispute is possible is because we do not always have a perfectly adequate, pretheoretical understanding of the value concepts we employ. When a dispute over the internality of a judgment emerges, there is only one way to resolve it: conceptual analysis. It is through conceptual analysis that a rough understanding of a value concept becomes more refined, and thus it is a tool that can be used to draw the boundary between judgments internal and external to a value with as much precision as possible.

Second, with respect to my objector's particular example, namely the example of utilitarian fairness, we need to be clear about the sense in which fairness and efficiency coincide here. On the one hand, it is true that implementing the utilitarian conception of fairness coincides with implementing a maximum average utility conception of efficiency. That utilitarianism is able to marry fairness and efficiency in this way makes it an aesthetically pleasing theory of morality. It is false, however, to say that a consequence of this marriage is the elimination of the distinction between fairness and efficiency. Equality of weight when promoting individuals' welfare, as a conception of fairness, and the maximization of average welfare, as a conception of efficiency, are still two different conceptions, and the values behind them are still two different values. As a result, one can consistently reject one of these conceptions and yet embrace the other. Consider the utilitarian understanding of fairness in particular, namely that a fair distribution is one that gives equal weight to the promotion of each person's welfare. We should still distinguish between considerations of fairness and efficiency when evaluating this conception, and it is specifically considerations of fairness that should be appealed to. For example, it might be thought that intuitive judgments about relative need support this conception. For example, those who are hungry get far more utility out of food than those who have had their fill, so would it not be unfair if we redistributed food in such a way that those who are hungry have little of it and those who are full have plenty? However, a bit of sustained reflection reveals that judgments about need often undermine this conception too, as needs can sometimes be very costly to meet. Someone with a severe congenital disability might require a great a deal of resources in order to function at the same level as those who are not disabled. Is it fair for someone born with such a disability to undergo the associated hardships without any help from the state? Most people would say that it is not, and yet that is not the result utilitarian fairness yields. If promoting a disabled individual's utility requires a large amount of resources,

resources that could be used to generate a greater amount of utility if distributed elsewhere, then utilitarian fairness would deprive the disabled individual of support. For some people, including myself, the judgment that it is unfair to neglect those with costly congenital disabilities serves as a decisive strike against the utilitarian conception of fairness.[35]

What about the maximum average utility conception of efficiency? When the utilitarian conception of fairness falls, does the maximum average utility conception of efficiency fall with it? Not necessarily. Efficiency is a value distinct from fairness. What is more, just as considerations of efficiency are external to fairness, so too are considerations of fairness external to efficiency. As a result, if maximizing the average amount of utility runs afoul of the above-mentioned disability objection, then it makes sense to say that it has unfair implications. Presumably, however, it would not make sense to judge either a distribution or a society to be inefficient because it neglects those with expensive needs. We should recall that the concept of efficiency pertains to increasing the amount of a good. Total aggregate happiness, gross domestic product: these are the sorts of measures we might use to evaluate a society's efficiency. Does maximum average utility serve as an adequate evaluative criterion in this respect? If we want to determine the extent to which maximum average utility is an adequate judge of a society's efficiency, then we should draw specifically on judgments of efficiency in order to make the evaluation. For example, if we wanted to decide between a maximum aggregate utility conception of societal efficiency and a maximum average utility conception of societal efficiency, then we might compare a society with a large aggregate but low average amount of utility, for example, one with a large population of miserable people, to a society with a high average but low aggregate utility, for example, one with a small population of happy people. Does it make sense to say that a society with a very large but generally miserable population is more efficient than a society with a fairly small but generally happy population? Presumably not, and yet a maximum aggregate utility conception of societal efficiency has this consequence. Understanding efficiency in terms of average instead of aggregate amount thus seems wise. The most obvious problem with using maximum average utility as a criterion to evaluate the efficiency of a society is with respect to the 'utility' part of it, I think, rather than the 'maximum average' part. This is because an impoverished society might nonetheless have a high average level of subjective welfare if its citizens have successfully adapted their preferences to their dismal circumstances. Yet to think of a society as efficient because its citizens have low expectations would be strange.[36] Thus, while I think it is plausible to understand efficiency in terms of maximum average amounts, I do not think it is plausible to equate the efficiency of a society's distribution of subjective welfare with the efficiency of the society itself. There are other goods that must be efficiently promoted as well in order for a society to be efficient on the whole.

By way of concluding remarks on the subjects of fairness and efficiency, I would like to point out that whether our conceptions of fairness and efficiency coincide or come apart has significant normative implications. If fairness and efficiency require the same thing in practice, such as maximizing the average amount, then even a radical value pluralist has a very powerful normative reason to pursue the maximization of whatever quantifiable good she thinks these values should be applied to. This reason might still be a defeasible one, but if the demands of fairness and efficiency exhaustively coincide, then it is likely that many of the competing considerations they could run up against will be trumped. The upshot for political practice would be that the content of the regulatory principles we adopt should be far more expressive of both fairness and efficiency than they otherwise would be. In contrast, if fairness and efficiency come apart such that they come into conflict with each other, then the extent to which either should be justifiably implemented in the content of our regulatory principles will be far more limited.

In future chapters, I assume that fairness and efficiency sometimes conflict. This assumption is partially grounded in my endorsement of a conception of fairness that sometimes conflicts with efficiency regardless of which understanding of efficiency one prefers. In Chapter 3, I will argue that the principle of luck equality supplies a compelling conception of fairness, and in Chapter 4, I will extensively discuss issues surrounding a contingent conflict between fairness and efficiency: a conflict associated with the character of a society's ethos.

Notes

1. See Cohen (2008) pp. 315–23; and Temkin (2002) pp. 154–5. For a discussion of the relationship between the levelling down objection, value pluralism, and G.A. Cohen's fact-insensitivity thesis, see Johannsen (2017).
2. Macleod (1998) pp. 115–6.
3. Christiano (2007) pp. 71–8.
4. I owe thanks to Will Kymlicka for this objection.
5. See, for example, Partfit (2002) p. 98.
6. See, for example, Christiano (2007) pp. 71–2. For an instance where an author uses the term 'levelling down' in both of the above-mentioned ways, see Temkin (2002) pp. 130–1.
7. Macleod (1998) pp. 112–4.
8. For my part, I am not sure that it would be inappropriate to say of a course of action that effectively and economically achieves some goal X that, even though it hampers the pursuit of some goal Y, it is nonetheless efficient specifically with respect to the pursuit of goal X. It strikes me that we might want to say of such an act that it is *globally inefficient*, that is, inefficient from the standpoint of the agent's entire network of goals, but nonetheless still *locally efficient*, that is, efficient with respect to the particular goal at which it aimed.
9. Macleod (1998) pp. 112–3.
10. I owe thanks to Alistair Macleod for (implicitly) suggesting that I use the term 'quantitative' to distinguish the sense of 'efficiency' I am interested in.
11. For a discussion that describes this concept nicely, albeit in an indirect fashion, see Waldron (2003) pp. 275–7.
12. See Rawls (1971) pp. 36–7 and pp. 66–7.
13. Rawls (1971) pp. 161–75.
14. Rawls (1971) p. 67.

15. I owe thanks to Christine Sypnowich for this particular objection.
16. Michael Stocker discusses the idea that some values are best understood as *functions*, that is, as specific sources of information about how an agent should act with respect to, or evaluate, morally significant, quantifiable goods. See Stocker (1997) pp. 202–3.
17. Waldron (2003) p. 277. Though Waldron uses the term 'justice' rather than 'fairness,' he is careful to note that he specifically has narrow justice in mind. Perhaps he would be fine with my using his account to characterize fairness. See Waldron's comments on page 274.
18. Waldron takes the same approach in his own discussion of fairness. See Waldron (2003) pp. 275–7.
19. Christiano (2007) pp. 71–8.
20. I owe thanks to Will Kymlicka for this objection.
21. Dworkin (2000) p. 1.
22. For a discussion of this problem, see Kymlicka (2002) pp. 32–7.
23. For Rawls's characterization of reflective equilibrium, see Rawls (1971) pp. 19–21 and pp. 46–53. For an excellent collection of essays on both the theorization and application of reflective equilibrium, see Daniels (1996).
24. Rawls (1971) pp. 47–50. See also Rawls (1974–75) p. 8.
25. Frankfurt (1971).
26. Frankfurt (1971) pp. 14–20.
27. See Hume (1993) pp. 53–69.
28. See, for example, G. Dworkin (1976); and Christman (1991).
29. G. Dworkin (1976) pp. 25–6.
30. For Cohen's comments on what he takes to be external to justice, see Cohen (2008) pp. 156–61 and pp. 315–36.
31. Though, as Christine Sypnowich points out, levelling down resources in particular can arguably have a number of benefits; for example, it can increases levels of trust and civility among citizens. See Sypnowich (2003) pp. 338–9.
32. See Cohen's comments in Cohen (2008) pp. 6–8 and pp. 300–2.
33. See Sen (1979) pp. 198–205; Dworkin (2000) pp. 62–4; and Kymlicka (2002) pp. 32–3.
34. Alistair Macleod has made similar points on one or more occasions when discussing how to go about doing philosophy.
35. See Sen (1979) pp. 202–5.
36. For a seminal analysis of adaptive preferences, see Elster (1982).

References

Christiano, Thomas. 2007. "A Foundation for Egalitarianism." In *Egalitarianism: New Essays on the Nature and Value of Equality*. Eds. Nils Holtug and Kasper Lippert-Rasmussen (New York: Clarendon Press).

Christman, John. 1991. "Autonomy and Personal History." *Canadian Journal of Philosophy* 21: 1–24.

Cohen, G.A. 2008. *Rescuing Justice and Equality* (Cambridge, MA: Harvard University Press).

Daniels, Norman. 1996. *Justice and Justification: Reflective Equilibrium in Theory and Practice* (Cambridge: Cambridge University Press).

Dworkin, Gerald. 1976. "Autonomy and Behavior Control." *Hastings Center Report* 6: 23–8.

Dworkin, Ronald. 2000. *Sovereign Virtue*: *The Theory and Practice of Equality* (Cambridge, MA: Harvard University Press). Pp. 65–119.

Elster, Jon. 1982. "Sour Grapes: Utilitarianism and the Genesis of Wants." In *Utilitarianism and Beyond*. Eds. Amartya Sen and Bernard Williams (Cambridge: Cambridge University Press). Pp. 219–38.

Frankfurt, Harry G. 1971. "Freedom of the Will and the Concept of a Person." *The Journal of Philosophy* 68: 5–20.

Hume, David. 1993. *An Enquiry Concerning Human Understanding*. Ed. Eric Steinberg (Indianapolis: Hackett Publishing).

Johannsen, Kyle. 2017. "On the Theoretical Significance of G.A. Cohen's Fact-Insensitivity Thesis." *Res Publica* 23(2): 245–53.

Kymlicka, Will. 2002. *Contemporary Political Philosophy: An Introduction* (New York: Oxford University Press).

Macleod, Alistair. 1998. "Efficiency and Justice." In "Law, Justice & Culture." *Arsp-Beiheft*. Vol. 68. Eds. Andre-Jean Arnaud & Peter Koller (Stuttgart: Franz Steiner). Pp. 111–9.

Parfit, Derek. 2002. "Equality or Priority?" In *The Ideal of Equality*. Eds. Matthew Clayton and Andrew Williams (New York: Palgrave-Macmillan). Pp. 81–125.

Rawls, John. 1971. *A Theory of Justice* (Cambridge, MA: Belknap Press).

Rawls, John. 1974–75. "The Independence of Moral Theory." *Proceedings and Addresses of the American Philosophical Association* 48: 5–22.

Sen, Amartya. May 22nd, 1979. "Equality of What?" *The Tanner Lecture on Human Values*. Stanford University. Pp. 197–220. Accessed on March 4th, 2015. Available at http://tannerlectures.utah.edu/_documents/a-to-z/s/sen80.pdf

Stocker, Michael. 1997. "Abstract and Concrete Value: Plurality, Conflict, and Maximization." In *Incommensurability, Incomparability, and Practical Reason*. Ed. Ruth Chang (Cambridge, MA: Harvard University Press).

Sypnowich, Christine. 2003. "From Marxism to Liberalism (and Back Again)." *Political Studies Review* 1: 333–43.

Temkin, Larry. 2002. "Equality, Priority, and the Levelling Down Objection." In *The Ideal of Equality*. Eds. Matthew Clayton and Andrew Williams (New York: Palgrave-Macmillan). Pp. 126–61.

Waldron, Jeremy. 2003. "The Primacy of Justice." *Legal Theory* 9: 269–94.

3 Defeasible Luck Equality

1. Introduction

Anti-egalitarians have long complained that egalitarianism fails to hold the less well-off responsible for the consequences of their choices. Implementing distributive equality requires redistributing to those who have less, but doesn't that entail subsidizing leisure seekers and bailing out the imprudent? According to luck egalitarianism, the answer to that question is an emphatic "no!" By focusing on the equalization of substantial opportunities in particular, luck egalitarianism makes it a requirement of equality that citizens be held responsible for the distributive consequences of their choices. As G. A. Cohen puts it when commenting on the first (Ronald Dworkin's) version of the theory, "Dworkin has, in effect, performed for egalitarianism the considerable service of incorporating within it the most powerful idea in the arsenal of the anti-egalitarian right: the idea of choice and responsibility."[1]

In recent years, however, luck egalitarianism has received a considerable amount of critical attention. According to its most prominent critics, luck egalitarianism conflicts with respect for citizens and is excessively harsh towards those who make imprudent choices.[2] To repel these and other objections, many luck egalitarians have replied that the principle of luck equality is defeasible: it represents a consideration that must be given weight in practical reasoning about politics, but it should also sometimes give way to competing considerations.[3] Is this resilience to criticism bought at too steep a price, though? According to Kok-Chor Tan, defeating objections by subjecting luck equality to trade-offs is a Pyrrhic victory.[4] Rarely are all things equal, so predicating defeasibility of luck equality makes it an unreliable guide to political action. If defending luck egalitarianism requires giving up its capacity for action guidance, then perhaps we are better off abandoning the theory all together.

The purpose of this chapter is to bring to light the merits of a defeasible luck egalitarian principle. As we will see, one of the virtues of defeasible luck equality is that it can indeed repel objections successfully. However, defeasibility is more than just a convenient way of replying to criticism. It also gives luck egalitarianism the capacity to recognize sources of unfairness that action-guiding principles are necessarily blind to. What's more, though a defeasible luck egalitarian principle is unsuitable to serve as a direct guide to political action, it nonetheless has the capacity to make a subtle but important contribution to practical reasoning about politics.

I begin this chapter by explaining the theoretical advantages and problems associated with luck egalitarianism. I suggest that luck egalitarianism's relative popularity among egalitarians is attributable to its coherence with certain core intuitive judgments, such as the judgment that it is unfair for one's endowment of natural talents to determine one's life prospects, the judgment that it is fair for those who choose leisure over work to have less than others, and so on.[5] I also go over the major criticisms critics have launched against luck egalitarianism in recent years, such as the criticism that it expresses a disrespectful attitude towards those it would seek to assist, that it treats victims of bad option luck with excessive harshness, and so on.[6]

In section 3, I explain why the aforementioned advantages are specifically advantages for a conception of a defeasible value and why the aforementioned problems are, in many cases, specifically problems for a theory of how we should design our institutions, all things considered. In support of my case, I draw on a distinction developed in the previous chapter: the distinction between the intuitive judgments relevant to justifying a conception of a value and the judgments relevant to justifying action-guiding principles. I argue that luck egalitarianism does a better job of cohering with the set of judgments belonging to the value that (many) luck egalitarians are attempting to theorize (I call it distributive fairness throughout), but a worse job of cohering with our all-things-considered judgments of right and wrong.

In section 4, I consider Ronald Dworkin's and Kok-Chor Tan's replies to the harshness objection, as they avoid sacrificing luck egalitarianism's capacity for action guidance.[7] I argue that even if these replies are successful, an action-guiding version of luck egalitarianism would not obviate the need for a distinct, defeasible version of the theory. By designing their theories to be action guiding, Tan and Dworkin render them incapable of capturing some clear cases of unfairness.

Finally, in section 5, I explain some of the practical functions of defeasible luck equality. One is that it can be used to rank our duties to those in need. As we will see, clarifying our priorities is normative specifically when it is not feasible to help everyone. Another function is that defeasible luck equality can inform factually contingent improvements to Rawls's difference principle. For example, I note that eliminating inequalities of opportunity traceable to membership in social and racial groups creates the conditions needed to implement a greater degree of fairness without sacrificing respect. Under these circumstances, it becomes morally preferable to distinguish between imprudent members of the worst-off class and those who are worst off through no fault of their own. Though a basic needs safety net should nonetheless be employed to safeguard the imprudent, I will argue that inequalities should maximally benefit only those whose worst-off status is traceable to sheer bad luck.

2. Luck Egalitarianism: For and Against

Originally given its name by critic Elizabeth Anderson,[8] luck egalitarianism, broadly speaking, is the view that inequalities traceable to choice are just, while those traceable to luck are not. Its proponents maintain that justice supports compensating a less well-off individual insofar as her disadvantaged status is no fault of her own.[9] Though this characterization makes the view sound rather simple, a number of theoretical complexities are associated with it. For instance, one might wonder how to address inequalities produced by choice and luck in combination, such as inequalities between those who intentionally expose themselves to risky situations. The distinction between option luck and brute luck speaks to this. Most luck egalitarians accept that the distributive effects of option luck (luck associated with deliberate gambles) are fair.[10] A second issue pertains to the metric of equality, particularly whether egalitarians should be concerned with luck's impact on resource possession, subjective welfare, or the attainment of something broader than either of these.[11]

Its theoretical complexities aside, understanding why luck egalitarianism is an appealing theory of justice is easier when it is compared to Rawls's theory.[12] For example, one area where Rawls's theory has been criticized is with regards to its ostensible neglect for those born with (or who accidentally acquire) disabilities. Though part of the justification for Rawls's difference principle is that it "mitigates the arbitrary effects of the natural lottery,"[13] it specifically focuses on the worst-off class and thus on mitigating the class-related effects of unequal natural ability. But do not inequalities in natural ability matter in other ways too? Ceteris paribus, a disabled member of the worst-off class is disadvantaged relative to a typically functioning member of that class (either by having lower welfare, extra material costs, or fewer physical resources), so should society not endow the disabled individual with additional compensatory benefits? Luck egalitarianism responds to this issue by acknowledging that disadvantages attributable to sheer misfortune, genetic or otherwise, are beyond the scope of responsibility and are thus unfair. For the luck egalitarian, considerations of fairness are in favor of compensating for the intra-class effects of unequal natural ability just as much as they are in favor of compensating for its inter-class effects.[14]

Another area where Rawls's theory has been criticized is for subsidizing the choices of those responsible for their own disadvantaged state. For example, some people prefer to gamble with their earnings, and others like having an abundance of leisure. Why would it be unfair for one to have fewer material resources for reasons like this? Is it not unfair for society to subsidize gamblers and leisure seekers with the earnings of those who have chosen to work hard and/or be prudent? Luck egalitarianism corrects for this deficiency by acknowledging that those who are worse off because of their choices are responsible for their status, while those worse off because they possess less natural talent are not. For the luck egalitarian, fairness prohibits subsidizing the gambler or the surfer and, at the same time, requires compensating those with less natural talent.[15]

Though the above considerations suggest that luck egalitarianism represents a clear improvement over Rawls's theory of justice, a number of egalitarian theorists have reacted negatively to it. They object that a form of egalitarianism that seeks to redress all and only inequalities beyond the scope of personal responsibility makes extravagant metaphysical assumptions about the nature of free will, expresses a disrespectful attitude towards those it would seek to assist, and has counter-intuitive implications.

According to Samuel Scheffler, any conception of justice that puts as much weight on the notion of choice as luck egalitarianism relies on a radical understanding of agency. The plausibility of claiming that a citizen's entitlement to compensation is entirely determined by whether or not her plight is traceable to choice requires that choice carry special significance. It is not enough to say that a decision was uncoerced. An agent whose decisions are uncoerced does not necessarily bear full responsibility for them, as there are a variety of circumstances that can sever the connection between choice and responsibility to various extents, such as misinformation, the effects of inebriation, temporary impairment caused by a bout of anger or depression, and so forth. Nor does it suffice to stipulate that luck egalitarianism is specifically concerned with holding people responsible for choices made under normal conditions. For even under normal conditions people's choices are involuntarily influenced by biological and social factors over which they lack control. According to Scheffler, the luck egalitarian is committed to an incompatibilist view of freedom that sees human decision makers as possessing the capacity to somehow transcend the influence of causal forces. Only someone who endorses incompatibilism could consistently claim that whether a disadvantage is or is not traceable to choice suffices to determine its compensability.[16] Though Scheffler concedes that the presence or absence of choice is a factor plausibly carrying some significance when determining the compensability of disadvantage, he maintains that it only has the 'make or break significance' luck egalitarians accord it if one accepts an implausible view of free will.[17]

Suppose we were to put the issue of free will aside and agreed, for the sake of argument or otherwise, that there is no metaphysical bar to making the presence or absence of choice the central consideration when determining whether compensation is justified. In order to secure a distribution consistent with luck egalitarian requirements, the state would have to go about acquiring the information necessary for making accurate interpersonal comparisons. But isn't this impossible? And even if it wasn't, wouldn't any attempt to accomplish it intrude intolerably on the privacy of citizens? Some of this worry applies only insofar as luck egalitarians include welfare within their metric, as collecting information about resource levels is easier to do without invading privacy than is collecting information about the extent to which preferences are satisfied.[18] However, luck egalitarianism's emphasis on choice makes even a resource metric vulnerable to the invasiveness charge, as it would be necessary to determine not only the extent to which resources are unequal, but also the extent to which individuals can properly be held responsible for inequalities.[19] As a result of worries about invasiveness, luck egalitarians have been careful from the beginning to point out that they do not mean to advocate privacy violations. Despite his opposition to resourcism, Richard Arneson indicates that the epistemic accessibility of resource levels might justify using them as rough proxies for welfare.[20] Similarly, Dworkin indicates that the impossibility of disentangling the portion of a person's resource level traceable to his circumstances from the portion traceable to his choices suggests modeling redistributive tax systems around the idea of a hypothetical insurance market. Such a tax system would strive to compensate a person for an instance of misfortune to the extent demanded by a hypothetical average coverage level set in light of factors such as a misfortune's severity, its likelihood of occurring, and the cost of compensation.[21]

Though a proposal such as Dworkin's requires less data collection than a straightforward attempt to track the precise impact of brute luck on citizens' lives, it would still require that the state have access to sensitive personal information. In particular, the state would need to know who has suffered from misfortune and what the nature of that misfortune was, even if knowledge of the precise impact of that misfortune on one's relative status is unnecessary. The most obvious way to collect such data without an invasive state surveillance system would be to make compensation conditional on the recipient's willingness to demonstrate that she's been afflicted by a form of bad luck. Though such a method is comparatively preferable, Jonathan Wolff has argued that it nonetheless has worrisome implications. Requiring disadvantaged citizens to prove their case ostensibly expresses a distrustful attitude. As if being a victim of misfortune was not bad enough by itself, conditional compensation adds insult to injury by treating claimants as objects of suspicion.

What's more, proving that one has suffered bad luck sometimes requires what Wolff calls "shameful revelation," that is, providing personal information, the disclosure of which would reasonably cause one to experience a sense of shame. An obvious example is the genetically unlucky being required to reveal lesser mental capacities, poor social skills, and so forth.[22] Even if the collection of data can be conducted in such a way as to avoid expressing distrust or requiring shameful revelation, Elizabeth Anderson insists that luck egalitarianism's very rationale is degrading for the recipients of compensation. For the state to award compensation to citizens on the basis of, say, their unfortunate lack of marketable talent or inferior social ability is to express pity towards them (specifically of the condescending variety expressed by someone who feels superior to another). Awarding compensation out of pity is damning for the theory, according to Anderson, as it suggests that luck egalitarianism is incompatible with respect for beneficiaries' dignity.[23]

If the above criticisms are to be taken seriously, then luck egalitarianism is in serious tension with respect for citizens. Good as luck egalitarianism is at capturing philosophers' intuitive judgments about fairness and unfairness in distribution, it allegedly does so at the cost of demeaning those whom it would seek to assist. Of course, it is possible for a luck egalitarian to bite the bullet here. She could perhaps argue that the theoretical benefits of luck egalitarianism outweigh whatever tension there might be between it and respect. According to Anderson and Scheffler, however, this move is not available. They claim that luck egalitarianism cannot even do what it is allegedly best at: namely, capture our intuitive judgments about particular cases of compensability. Scheffler indicates that it is not hard to think of cases where compensation would be counterintuitive and yet still required by luck egalitarianism. Consider, for instance, cases where people achieve differential levels of success due to differential talents. Would it be unjust for a naturally gifted philosopher to be more successful at her job then a less-gifted colleague? Would it be unjust for a gifted athlete to receive greater reward than a less-gifted one? Scheffler thinks most people's intuitions run contrary to the luck egalitarian's in these cases.[24]

Similarly, both Scheffler and Anderson indicate that luck egalitarianism's emphasis on holding people responsible for the outcomes of their choices is excessively harsh. Even when a person can be properly held responsible for the problems that befall her, most people would agree that the state should assist those whose risky behavior or lack of prudence has landed them in dire circumstances. Should, for instance, negligent drivers be denied emergency care when injured in car accidents? Should someone whose poor financial decisions land her in extreme poverty be denied the financial assistance necessary to meet her basic needs? When cases like these are considered alongside those mentioned above, it seems to follow that luck egalitarianism compensates those it should not and fails to compensate those it should.[25]

In light of all this, critics of luck egalitarianism propose that egalitarians are better off focusing on a society's relational character, rather than on its distributive character. Instead of asking whether a society's citizens have equal access to X, they suggest we inquire into the manner in which they relate to each other. Is the society we are assessing one in which citizens relate to each other as members of equal status? Or are some relegated to a subordinate position and treated as inferiors? Supporting a society characterized by egalitarian relations between social groups requires opposing oppression and class hierarchy, not equalizing the distributive impact of luck. Of course, luck egalitarianism's critics do not typically eschew distributive considerations entirely. The general consensus seems to be that creating a society of equals would require some degree of redistribution, such as a social minimum sufficient to ensure that no one would be vulnerable to economic exploitation, for instance. Insofar as redistribution is desirable, however, it is on the basis of its instrumental contribution to a society where people relate to each other as equals, rather than on the basis of a distributive pattern's intrinsic significance.[26]

3. A Defense of Defeasible Luck Egalitarian Justice; a Rejection of All-Things-Considered Luck Egalitarian Justice

(a) The Appeal of Luck Egalitarianism: One-Thing-Considered, not All-Things-Considered

In the previous section, I sought to explain two things: (a) why many theorists have found luck egalitarianism to be an appealing theory, and (b) the reasons other theorists have offered for rejecting it. In this section, I will use the theoretical resources developed in Chapter 2 to analyze both the advantages and criticisms I have canvassed. I will argue that understanding luck egalitarianism as a conception of a defeasible value—specifically distributive fairness—helps us to better understand the sense in which it is an improvement over Rawls's theory. I will also argue that it helps us to see why many of the above-described criticisms are only effective when luck egalitarianism is (mistakenly, on my view) put forward as a theory of institutional rightness.

It has recently come to light that Rawlsians and (many) luck egalitarians are not using the word 'justice' in the same way.[27] In his 2006 commentary on G. A. Cohen's version of luck egalitarianism, Thomas Scanlon notes that Cohen's 'equal access to advantage' seems primarily to be a thesis about the conditions states of affairs must satisfy in order to qualify as just, whereas Rawls is primarily interested in determining how we should design our institutions. Scanlon also notes that insofar as Cohen's luck egalitarianism does bear on institutions, it is specifically about how they should be designed, all things being equal, from the perspective of equality. Rawls, by contrast, is interested in the somewhat different question of how institutions should be designed, all things considered. Scanlon concludes that, in spite of the fact that Cohen and Rawls both use the term 'justice,' their theories are addressing different, albeit related questions.[28]

In his book *Rescuing Justice and Equality*, Cohen picks up where Scanlon leaves off, adding further content to the description of how his use of the word 'justice' differs from Rawls's. He explains that what he's referring to with the word 'justice' is a defeasible value. This value is one of the normative *inputs* involved in the justificatory process via which action guiding institutional principles are selected, rather than the *output*.[29] Cohen's use of the word implies a pluralistic picture of the meta-ethical universe. For pluralists like him, morality is composed of a plurality of irreducible, defeasible values that sometimes conflict with each other.[30] As a result, any principle expressing the content of a value, such as a principle of efficiency, a principle of publicity, a principle of community (fraternity), and so on, is only indirectly normative on a pluralist view. Such a principle tells us how to evaluate a society with respect to one of the moral elements in light of which it is or isn't morally desirable, but it cannot by itself tell a legislator what to *do*.[31] To identify justice as a value, then, is to identify it as a tool directly useful for evaluating the extent to which a society is fair but only indirectly useful for telling us how a society ought to be run.

Rawlsians, by contrast, are interested in the output of practical reasoning about how to design our shared institutions. The principles their theoretical efforts aim at are what Cohen calls 'rules of regulation,' that is, derived, context-specific principles that function as guides to action. When justice is understood as an output, articulating a theory of justice requires taking into account a lot of normative information. With respect to considerations of desirability, values to be considered in addition to fairness when adopting regulatory principles include efficiency, publicity, and community. With respect to feasibility, regulatory principles must reflect considerations of *accessibility*, that is, considerations pertaining to the possibility of implementing a set of regulatory principles, as well as considerations of *stability*, that is, considerations pertaining to the sustainability of the regulatory principles being proposed for adoption.[32]

It could be argued that Cohen is idiosyncratic: a one-off luck egalitarian whose view does not accurately represent the luck egalitarian position more generally. As we will see in the next section, some luck egalitarians, namely Ronald Dworkin and Kok-Chor Tan, refuse to regard the moral requirements of their theories as defeasible. Whether they are talking about something different from Cohen is a question worth asking. This complication aside, though, the claim that at least *many* luck egalitarians are using the word 'justice' differently than Rawls is confirmed by much of the luck egalitarian literature. If we look at Richard Arneson's canonical paper on the subject, it is clear that he took 'equal opportunity for welfare' to be a conception of a defeasible value. When discussing the problem of compensation for religious preferences, he claims that "even if we all agree that in such cases a policy of compensation is inappropriate, all things considered, it does not follow that so far as distributive equality is concerned (one among the several values we cherish), compensation should not be forthcoming."[33] Additionally, in recent work luck egalitarians have used value pluralism to defend against criticisms like the harshness objection. They argue that values such as a humanitarian concern for the satisfaction of basic needs or a community-based concern for the well-being of co-citizens require striking a compromise with luck equality in practice.[34]

In Chapter 2, I argued that the method via which one arrives at a conception of a value is similar to, but also importantly different from, reflective equilibrium. When using reflective equilibrium to justify a set of action-guiding principles, the goal is to ensure coherence with our particular intuitions about what is right or wrong, all things considered. Justifying a conception of a value, in contrast, involves drawing upon a narrower set of intuitive judgments. One must first be attentive to distinguishing between intuitive judgments internal to the value in question from those external to it, as the goal is to achieve coherence specifically with those internal to it. When offering a conception of distributive fairness, the intuitive judgments with which one is concerned are specifically judgments about what is fair or unfair, rather than judgments that belong to other values, such as judgments about what would count as autonomous or non-autonomous, compassionate or harsh, and so forth. They are also judgments that, in some cases, will only hold in the ceteris paribus sense of 'ought.' This is important. Some of our judgments of fairness, such as that it is unfair for employers to discriminate against applicants on the basis of irrelevant physical characteristics (such as eye color), are normatively robust. Other values tend not to conflict with them in most cases or, if they do, they are usually trumped by the value of fairness. As a result, the truth of the judgment that it is *unfair* to discriminate against applicants on the basis of irrelevant physical characteristics tends to successfully entail the judgment that it is *wrong* to do so. Other judgments, such as that it's unfair for society to subsidize the imprudent, are less robust. In severe cases, this judgment is trumped by the importance of alleviating severe suffering and meeting basic needs. As such, the judgment that it is *unfair* to subsidize the imprudent frequently fails to justify the claim that it is *wrong* to do so. The fact that this judgment of fairness lacks normative robustness, though, does not mean that it should be put aside when attempting to articulate a conception of distributive fairness. When articulating such a conception in matters of distribution, the goal is to formulate a criterion the satisfaction of which is necessary and sufficient for a distribution to count as fair. Insofar as there are cases that *do not* satisfy our criterion yet we judge to be fair, then our criterion is vulnerable to counter-examples that challenge its adequacy as a *necessary* condition. Insofar as there are cases that *do* satisfy our criterion yet we judge to be unfair, then our criterion is vulnerable to counter-examples that challenge its adequacy as a *sufficient* condition.

Leaving out the judgment that it is unfair to subsidize the imprudent would have the latter effect. Any principle of distributive fairness that does not evaluate such cases as unfair is open to the charge that its satisfaction does not suffice to guarantee the fairness of a distribution. Of course, a justice theorist whose goal is something other than to provide a necessary and sufficient criterion might have reason to put this judgment aside when formulating her conception, at least in cases where the imprudent are in dire need. Doing so is wise if one's goal is the rather different goal of delineating the boundaries of fairness's capacity for action-guidance. I discuss this further in section 4.

When luck egalitarianism's theoretical advantages over Rawls's theory of justice are understood in light of the above, it becomes clear that those advantages are of a very specific kind. By failing to distinguish those of the worst-off whose disadvantaged status is traceable to choice, and by failing to recognize that the unfairness of disabilities acquired by accident or at birth extends beyond their effect on socioeconomic class, Rawls's theory fails to adequately represent all our intuitive judgments of fairness. As a result, it fails to provide an adequate account of what distributive fairness is. Whether it fails to deliver an adequate account of how we should structure our institutions, all-things-considered (including fairness), is left open, though. After all, just because his theory fails to cohere with all our judgments of fairness does not mean that it fails to incorporate them as much as an action-guiding theory of institutional design reasonably can.

Likewise, just because luck egalitarianism does a better job of capturing our full range of fairness intuitions, and thus of telling us what distributive fairness is, does not mean that it does a better job of telling us how we should structure our institutions, all things considered. Cohering with our full range of fairness judgments includes cohering with judgments that may, upon reflection, fail to be normatively robust, a consequence of which is that a compelling conception of distributive fairness will tend not to be a compelling conception of institutional rightness. As I will now proceed to argue, many (but not all) of the objections to luck egalitarianism I canvassed in the previous section show exactly this: that luck egalitarianism is not a very good conception of institutional rightness. In what follows, I will address, one by one, the following problems: counter-intuitive cases invoked by Scheffler and Anderson where luck egalitarianism allegedly requires compensation where it should withhold it and withholds compensation where it should be required, Scheffler's worry about an implausible conception of freewill, Anderson's concern about the expression of pity, Wolff's problems of distrust and 'shameful revelations,' and the claim that luck egalitarianism focuses on distribution at the expense of social relationships.

(b) Counter-Intuitive Implications

Let's start with the charge that luck egalitarianism inappropriately requires compensation in some cases. According to Scheffler, luck egalitarianism implies that it is unfair for some members of the same profession to be naturally better at it than other members. He also claims that luck egalitarianism implies that differentially rewarding members of the same profession is unfair when the differential performance upon which the reward is based is due to differences of natural talent. The problem with these implications, according to Scheffler, is that most people find them counter-intuitive. Most people accept that it is fair for better philosophers to receive more accolades than their less-talented colleagues or for faster runners to be awarded larger trophies than slower runners. According to Scheffler, luck egalitarianism is less intuitively compelling than its proponents think.[35]

I am willing to grant that the cases Scheffler discusses are counter-intuitive. The problem with them is that they are bad examples of brute luck. In a society with freedom of occupation, inequalities between members of a particular profession are bound up with the choice to pursue that profession. As a result, a person who chooses to pursue a profession for which she is sub-optimally suited can, if she had access to the relevant information and the opportunity to pursue other professions for which she is well-suited, be held responsible for her lesser success. Suppose we were to change the example, though. Suppose we live in a society where professions are not chosen but are instead randomly assigned through a lottery mechanism. Such a society's infringement on liberty aside, would it be fair for a professional lucky enough to possess talents well-suited to the career she was assigned to fare better in life than her colleagues? Most people would say "no," and that is precisely the answer a luck egalitarian would want them to give. Of course, cases of occupational success and failure usually fall somewhere in between these two extremes (between full control and no control over one's profession). Intuitions will vary across such cases, but in all of them, I think said variance will track the extent to which choice accounts for the inequality. For example, inequality of success between two members of the same profession seems fair if one of those members does not care enough about her professional life to have put much thought into selecting a career her talents are suited to. It also seems fair if the difference between the two is attributable to the extent to which they choose to devote themselves to their work. In contrast, the difference seems unfair if each person was equally careful about selecting a career suited to her abilities and devotes an equal amount of time and effort to her work. In the first two cases, choice plays a big role in accounting for the relevant inequalities; hence they seem fair. In the last case, choice plays a much more limited role in accounting for the relevant inequality; hence it does not seem fair. All of this is perfectly consistent with luck egalitarianism.[36]

Let's consider another counter-intuitive implication: abandonment of the imprudent. By now, it should be clear what my reply is. I do not deny that luck egalitarianism implies it is unfair to subsidize the imprudent. I also do not deny that it would be counter-intuitive to let unsuccessful high-stakes gamblers starve, negligent drivers die by the side of the road, and so forth. I just do not think that the intuitions behind the harshness objection are intuitions of *fairness*. If anything, *compassion* for the imprudent is what accounts for the judgment that they ought not to be abandoned (hence why it is the 'harshness objection' rather than the 'unfairness objection'). That compassion should sometimes trump fairness is not surprising. However, it would be a mistake to conclude that compassion is generally weightier than fairness. In many cases of conflict, fairness is the value that wins out. For example, it would be absurd to say that the state should rush to my aid because I have a mild stomach ache from eating too much junk food or, if you don't like welfare metrics, that it should top up my back account because I blew all my disposable income for the week on a crate of non-refundable corn chips. It is appropriate for people to feel sorry when they see me grimacing with discomfort or when they find out that I have had to miss out on some fun social event or another because I can no longer afford to buy tickets, but that is it. Despite the appropriateness of feeling sorry for me, it would be unfair to others if public funds were spent to subsidize my junk food–related choices, and that unfairness successfully translates into wrongness in this case.

The cases discussed by proponents of the harshness objection, in contrast, are far more severe. They are cases that involve considerable suffering and/or an inability to satisfy basic needs. In severe cases like these, it is appropriate to feel *very* sorry for the imprudent, sorry enough to put aside considerations of fairness and provide aid to the point where a basic-needs threshold has been restored. Of course, there may also be other reasons for aid too. For example, it might damage a society's sense of 'solidarity' or 'community' were it to ignore the needs of imprudent members.[37] Compassion, however, is the most intuitively immediate value at play.

Before moving on to the next sub-section, I would like to address a problem Anderson raises for the implementation of state aid to the imprudent. The most obvious way to feasibly aid the imprudent in cases severe enough to warrant it is through a policy of compulsory contribution to public safety-net programs that provide unconditional service to those who need it. According to Anderson, however, luck egalitarians are unable to justify this approach without resorting to paternalistic reasoning. Since they are committed to holding people responsible for the outcomes of their choices, luck egalitarians are therefore allegedly against aiding those who choose to opt out of public safety-net programs and subsequently find themselves in dire straits. The rationale for compulsory participation would therefore have to be that the state should paternalistically prevent citizens from putting themselves in a position where it could not justifiably assist them, that is, that it should protect citizens from themselves by prohibiting them from risking their basic needs.[38]

A convenient response to Anderson is available to luck egalitarians who understand their view to be a conception of a defeasible value. They can claim that she incorrectly assumes luck egalitarians are unable to accept a duty to provide aid to needy opt-outers. Why does Anderson assume this? She assumes this because she also assumes that the luck egalitarian conception of justice is intended to be regulatory and thus that the principle of luck equality is not supposed to be defeasible. Once we have identified and dismissed her assumption about luck egalitarianism's theoretical status, though, the justificatory terrain around compulsory participation changes. Despite the unfairness of aiding imprudent individuals who have chosen to opt out of safety-net programs, luck egalitarians who understand luck egalitarianism as a conception of distributive fairness would still, out of deference to compassion, provide aid. They just prefer to set up state programs in such a way that the requirement to tolerate such unfairness need never arise. If participation in safety-net programs is made mandatory, then the tension between compassion and fairness is minimized, as there would not be any needy opt-outers to aid. For luck egalitarians of the stripe I am defending, a fairness rationale for compulsory participation is therefore available. Their rationale is not about preventing citizens from exposing themselves to risk, but rather about mitigating the exploitation of the prudent by requiring that the imprudent contribute too. Though the imprudent would receive aid regardless of whether they participate in safety-net programs, it is comparatively less unfair to aid imprudent contributors than it is to aid imprudent opt-outers. Thus a policy that makes participation mandatory yields more fairness than a policy that makes participation optional.[39]

(c) An Implausible Conception of Freewill

The most obvious advantage of interpreting luck egalitarianism as a conception of a defeasible value is that it corrects for the normative excess associated with treating luck equality as if it were the only thing that mattered for purposes of determining citizens' entitlements. As noted above, compassion, among other things, must be taken into account, too. An additional advantage associated with this interpretation of luck egalitarianism is that it addresses the metaphysical worry expressed by Scheffler. As noted earlier, Scheffler worries that treating the presence or absence of choice as a decisive criterion for justified redistribution presupposes an implausible picture of agency. He notes that on any compatibilist view of agency, a person's choices are acknowledged to be part of the same causal network that determines the circumstances she finds herself in. What makes a choice free on such a view is not insulation from external causal forces, but rather its relationship with the agent's values or second-order preferences (in an internalist view), the absence of a special class of agency undermining influences (in an externalist view), or a combination of both.[40] Regardless of the particular compatibilist account endorsed, though, once one acknowledges that both the motivational springs of action and the circumstances one finds oneself in are determined by external causal forces, according 'make or break' normative significance to choice seems unreasonable. Put another way, if the distinction between choice and circumstance is not a sharp one, then why should shortfalls traceable to choice be decisively exempt from compensation, while those traceable to circumstance decisively warrant it? Though a compatibilist can still say that the imprudent are responsible for the disadvantages incurred by their behavior, the sense in which a compatibilist would hold the imprudent responsible is more watered down than the sense in which a metaphysical libertarian, that is, someone who thinks autonomous actions are independent of external causes, would. In Scheffler's view, then, it is not sensible for a compatibilist to accord the choice/circumstance distinction too much weight in practical reasoning.[41]

Though I imagine Scheffler would not want to say that the truth of metaphysical libertarianism would suffice to justify luck egalitarianism (his metaphysical objection is only one among several), he does seem to think that it is necessary. As we have seen, however, interpreting luck egalitarianism as a conception of one value among many involves rejecting the claim that it has decisive normative significance. The presence of choice is considered to be a reason against compensation, and the absence of choice is considered to be a reason for compensation, but neither is a uniquely decisive reason. Instead, luck equality is seen as a defeasible consideration, one that must be given weight when adopting institutional regulatory principles but which must also be compromised insofar as it is reasonable to defer to the values luck equality conflicts with. As a result, the defender of defeasible luck equality need not exert herself when replying to Scheffler. It suffices to point out that the free will criticism doesn't apply on this understanding of what luck egalitarianism is a conception of, as the free will criticism presupposes that luck equality is supposed to be normatively decisive, rather than defeasible.

(d) Expressing Respect

Between Anderson and Wolff, the claim that luck egalitarianism is in tension with respect for persons has received a considerable amount of argumentative support. However, the criticisms each offers are sufficiently dissimilar to warrant separate treatment. Let's start with Anderson. As explained in the previous section, Anderson maintains that the luck egalitarian rationale for redistribution expresses pity (of the condescending sort) towards the disadvantaged. It allegedly implies that those with fewer natural gifts have "lives less worth living,"[42] and that they "lay claim to the resources of egalitarian distribution in virtue of their inferiority to others."[43] However, as Carl Knight correctly points out, Anderson's criticism is straightforwardly untrue.[44] Luck egalitarianism is not motivated by the thought that the unattractive, unintelligent, or socially inept are inferiors who warrant pity. Quite the opposite: luck egalitarianism is concerned with unchosen inequalities between persons of equal moral significance. It is precisely because people are moral equals with valuable interests that it is unfair for some to be worse off than others through no fault of their own.[45] Luck egalitarianism thus explicitly discourages the thought that those badly off with respect to natural gifts are 'inferior' in any morally significant sense of the word to those with an abundance of natural gifts.

Let's move on to Wolff. As we noted in section 2 of this chapter, Wolff suggests that there are serious concerns associated with the collection of data needed to make the interpersonal comparisons required for implementing luck egalitarianism. Even if luck egalitarians were to refrain from involuntary invasions of privacy, subjecting claimants to a screening process seems to express distrust at best and, at worst, requires the revelation of sensitive personal details that may be a source of shame for them. However, a close reading of Wolff reveals that his criticisms were never intended to suggest that luck egalitarianism is wrong.[46] His point, rather, was to draw attention to its normative limitations, that is, to specify some of the ways in which its implementation should be qualified. As he makes clear in the "Egalitarian Methodology" section of his seminal article, luck equality does a great job of capturing our intuitions about fairness in distribution. By employing the choice/circumstance distinction, luck egalitarians provide a rationale for why it is unfair for some to do better than their co-citizens by virtue of their natural talents or for some to do worse due to disability or the misfortune of being born into a lower class. Conversely, they are also able to explain why inequalities generated by lifestyle differences are fair, such as the inequality between a full-time surfer and a full-time mason, and thus why eliminating those inequalities through redistribution is not fair (at least when those inequalities reflect genuine choice).

When generalizing our intuitions about cases of this sort into a principle, however, the content of the principle produced omits important normative information relevant to guiding public policy.[47] Though Wolff is especially concerned with respect, other information is absent as well, such as a concern for efficiency as well as for the alleviation of suffering and satisfaction of basic needs. An appreciation for the information luck equality leaves out is important because attempts to implement a fair distribution must be sensitive to the moral costs potentially associated with doing so. In some cases, costs are associated with bad strategies for implementation and thus can largely be avoided by exercising a bit of ingenuity. For example, Wolff now acknowledges that methods of data collection capable of mitigating the experience of shame are available, such as sensitive interviews conducted in such a way as to draw special attention to what the claimant is good at while also screening out those whose disadvantaged state is traceable to choice.[48]

In other cases, costs are associated with contingent social circumstances, and thus policies that reflect an appropriate balancing of considerations are required for the moment but will not necessarily be required in the future. For example, Wolff is clear that he considers his worry about distrust to be a socially contingent one. He thinks that in our presently unjust state of affairs, the burden of having to reveal personal information would largely fall on members of the lower class, many (but not all) of whom are significantly disadvantaged through no fault of their own. Considering that the members of this group are already bearing the lion's share of society's burdens, it stands to reason that subjecting them to a disproportionately large amount of scrutiny would be experienced as disrespectful. In a society that already possesses a more or less luck egalitarian distribution, however, the burden of revealing personal information would not be distributed the same way. Since the involuntary inequalities associated with class hierarchy and racial discrimination will already have been eliminated, promoting justice would not require subjecting any particular social or racial group to excessive scrutiny.[49] This suggests that society should initially provide more in the way of unconditional benefits than it otherwise would until it has reached a stage where scrutiny would not be primarily focused on a particular social group.

Of course, some cases are not socially contingent. Some cases of value conflict are not just unavoidable at present but will presumably remain so regardless of the policies we implement. It will always be unfair to compensate a person whose inability to meet her basic needs is the product of genuine choice. Failing to do so, however, will also always infringe upon a society's obligation to ensure even its imprudent citizens are able to live a minimally decent life. Given the permanence of this conflict, policies that reflect an appropriate balance, such as mandatory safety-net programs, are unavoidable.[50]

(e) Distributive Equality vs. Social Equality[51]

Thus far, the present section of this chapter has analyzed the major criticisms of luck egalitarianism on offer. Though I have argued that some of them are just bad criticisms, in many cases I have claimed that their effectiveness depends on what luck egalitarianism is understood to be a theory of. On the one hand, if luck egalitarianism is understood as a theory of institutional rightness, then many of the criticisms it faces seem compelling. On the other hand, if it is understood as a theory of distributive fairness, then said criticisms lose their bite. Harshness, conflict with respect, and the metaphysical dullness of the distinction between choice and circumstance all limit the extent of the sway luck equality should have over the action-guiding principles we choose to adopt. They do not, however, impinge upon luck egalitarianism's adequacy as an account of the content of distributive fairness.

In this sub-section, I address the theoretical alternative critics of luck egalitarianism typically advocate: social equality. According to these critics, luck egalitarians are wrong about more than just the content of distributive fairness.

They also misunderstand the relationship between societal justice and matters of distribution. More specifically, advocates of social equality maintain that matters of distribution are specifically of instrumental significance to the justice of a society. A certain degree of redistribution from the well-off to the less well-off is needed to, for example, ensure that everyone is protected from domination and economic exploitation, but the feature that constitutes a just society is not its pattern of distribution. They claim that the constitutive feature is the quality of its social relations. On this view, a just society is one in which citizens relate to each other as equals. When describing her own proposed alternative to luck egalitarianism, Anderson writes that ". . . democratic equality is what I shall call a relational theory of equality, it views equality as a social relationship. . . . democratic equality regards two people as equal when each accepts the obligation to justify their actions by principles acceptable to the other, and in which they take mutual consultation, reciprocation, and recognition for granted."[52] For someone interested in social equality, then, the main thing justice theorists should be concerned with is the elimination of class hierarchy. What is objectionable about a society with a large amount of distributive inequality is not inequality in the distribution of goods per se, but rather the hierarchical class structure that tends to go along with it. When a particular social group has a monopoly over the wealth and power within a society, the result is a deformation of the relationship between it and other groups. Members of the upper-class group come to see themselves as superiors to whom deference is owed, while members of the other classes come to see themselves as inferiors, a consequence of which is damage to their sense of self-respect.[53] It is this deformation of social relations that proponents of social equality claim to be fundamentally concerned with.

Critics of luck egalitarianism are of course right to claim that social equality is of crucial significance to the justice of a society. The issue is not whether social equality is significant, but whether distributive equality has the comparative insignificance they claim it does. In reply to the claim that distributive equality, unlike social equality, is of instrumental significance, I have two points to make. First, implicit within this claim is a conceptual separation between distributive equality on the one hand and social equality on the other. Is there really a rigid conceptual distinction between these two kinds of equality? Perhaps there would be if distributive equality were strictly concerned with the distribution of wealth. As anyone with even a cursory level of familiarity with the literature knows, however, theories of distributive justice rarely target wealth alone.

Rawls, for instance, is concerned with a wide variety of social goods. Among other things, he is concerned with self-respect, a good that he acknowledges to be "perhaps the most important primary good."[54] In Rawls's view, the realization of self-respect requires (a) having a rational plan of life and (b) having a social relationship where the self-worth of those in the relationship is confirmed by those with whom they associate.[55] Admittedly, the idea that self-respect is a good to be distributed probably struck at least some of Rawls's readers as being a bit weird. It is thus not surprising to see a change of language in *Justice as Fairness: A Restatement*. There, he claims that institutions are to distribute "the social bases of self-respect, understood as those aspects of basic institutions normally essential if citizens are to have a lively sense of their worth as persons and to be able to advance their ends with confidence."[56] This minor adjustment notwithstanding, once we allow for a metric that possesses the kind of heterogeneity Rawls's does, it is no longer so clear that social equality is conceptually distinct from distributive equality. What would it mean for a society to have social equality but not an equal distribution of the social bases of self-respect, or, conversely, for a society to achieve an equal distribution of the social bases of self-respect but not social equality? The possibility that certain goods are constitutive of social equality undermines the implicit claim that social equality is separable from the distributive paradigm it allegedly challenges.

What's more, switching critical attention from a resource metric to something more fundamental (e.g., a welfare metric, a flourishing metric, etc.) does not do the advocate of social equality any good. If anything, understanding distributive equality in terms of equal welfare or flourishing reverses the alleged relationship between it and social equality; that is, it becomes the case that social equality has instrumental significance for the realization of distributive equality, rather than the other way around. This finding is inadvertently confirmed by Scheffler in his efforts to explain why social equality matters, for he notes that a major problem with socially inegalitarian societies is that they "compromise human flourishing: they limit personal freedom, corrupt human relationships, undermine self-respect, and inhibit truthful living."[57]

For the sake of argument, let us put aside the worries I express above. Let us grant that there is indeed a clear distinction between social and distributive equality. Furthermore, let us grant that the relationship between these kinds of equality is such that redistribution is instrumental to the realization of egalitarian social relationships. Even if we grant these points, it should be noted there is a big difference between instrumental significance and *mere* instrumental significance. Though I agree that the distribution of certain goods, such as wealth, has an instrumental relationship with the elimination of class hierarchy, I also think it is a mistake to say that a society's pattern of distribution is not part of what constitutes its justness. After all, a hypothetical society that somehow managed to implement social equality without also attending to matters of distribution would still be an unjust one. As Will Kymlicka rhetorically asks in his commentary on the subject, ". . . is it really unimportant that some people live in spacious houses while others are in cramped apartments; or that some people can afford month-long vacations overseas while others cannot afford to eat out at a local restaurant; or that some people have rewarding and fulfilling 'careers' while others have mind-numbing 'jobs', if they have a job at all?"[58] To say that these factors are merely of instrumental significance is implausible. We care about distributive equality not only because of its instrumental relationship with social equality, but also because of its constitutive relationship with the justice of a society.

The arguments I make above hopefully suffice to undermine the claim that social equality, and not distributive equality, is what's really essential to a just society. Before closing this sub-section, though, I would like to make note of two ways in which defeasible luck equality is especially well-equipped to handle social equality. As we have repeatedly noted, defeasible luck equality is embedded within a pluralistic framework: it sees fairness as one defeasible value among a plurality of defeasible values. It therefore acknowledges that values other than justice must be accorded weight when trying to achieve an all-things-considered optimal society. Some of these values, such as efficiency, are not specifically about the character of a society's social relations. Others, however, are.

A good example is 'community' or 'solidarity.' Community, as Cohen understands it, is a social relation that obtains when "people care about, and, where necessary and possible, care for, one another, and, too, care that they care about one another."[59] In fact, Cohen claims that maintaining this social relation is important enough to set a limit on the extent to which the imprudent should bear the costs of their choices. To illustrate how luck equality and community can come into conflict, he discusses the ways in which having ten times more wealth than someone else impedes a shared sense of community with that person. Part of the difficulty is that radical inequality like this entails that the individuals in question will lead qualitatively very different lives, that is, lives characterized by difficulties that only one of the parties will have to endure and luxuries that only the other can access. The idea here, I think, is that developing and maintaining a sense of mutual care is difficult when the pleasures and problems they face in their daily lives are of such a different character and magnitude.[60] Also of significance, though, is the fact that the richer individual has the means to provide assistance, but refrains from doing so. Since caring for the significantly less well-off individual is an option made possible by the better-off individual's possession of greater wealth, it is clear that permitting the former person to fully suffer the consequences of bad option luck stifles the motivations that constitute community.

Once it is acknowledged that proponents of defeasible luck equality are, among other things, concerned with realizing community, the claim that they ignore the character of a society's social relations becomes even more implausible. Community is straightforwardly concerned with social relations, as it is constituted by an attitude of mutual care for one another. In fact, the realization of a sense of 'solidarity' is one of the goods Scheffler points to when trying to explain the value of social equality.[61] Community is not the only value that bears upon the attitudes citizens have towards one another, however. So too does fairness, and part of what makes a society fair is the character of its *ethos*.[62] In Cohen's view, a society is not fully fair unless people care about whether their co-citizens have a fair share and are to some extent motivated to act upon that attitude. In the next chapter, I discuss the application of distributive fairness to the context of personal choice, and though I reject the claim that Rawls's difference principle extends to that context, I nonetheless maintain that fairness requires adopting other action-guiding distributive principles for personal decision making. If the arguments I present there are sound, then the claim that luck egalitarianism neglects social relations is even further challenged.

4. Alternative Defenses of Luck Egalitarianism

In the previous section, I defended luck egalitarianism against the most prominent criticisms of it. Among other things, I argued that a number of major criticisms, though seemingly effective against a theory of institutional rightness, lose their bite when the theory under assault is understood as a conception of a defeasible value, specifically distributive fairness. What's more, I argued that defeasible luck equality is uniquely well-equipped to deal with the charge that luck egalitarians are mistaken in choosing to focus upon distributive rather than social equality. Despite the benefits of understanding luck egalitarianism as a conception of a defeasible value, not all of its proponents would be comfortable with the distance such an understanding puts between luck egalitarianism and action guidance. If luck equality is defeasible, then the fact that implementing it requires a particular political course of action does not suffice to justify that course of action. Other normative considerations must also be taken into account before a final judgment is made. Seeing this as an unacceptable concession, Kok-Chor Tan and Ronald Dworkin have offered responses to the harshness objection that permit an action-guiding role for luck egalitarianism.[63] The possible success of these replies raises an important challenge to the understanding I've sketched. Might a version of luck egalitarianism suitably qualified along the lines suggested by either Tan or Dworkin obviate the need to interpret it as a conception of a defeasible value? As you might have guessed, my answer is 'no.' Before I explain why, though, I will briefly explain the defenses Tan and Dworkin offer.

Tan's response to the harshness objection relies upon a commonly accepted distinction in the global justice literature between duties of justice and duties of humanity.[64] The former require eliminating inequalities between the advantaged and the disadvantaged. The latter require redistribution in cases of poverty for the sake reaching a suitably defined sufficiency threshold, but do not require any redistribution beyond that point.[65] Much of the global justice literature is concerned with the issue of whether or not duties of humanity exhaust the distributive obligations owed by the global advantaged to the global disadvantaged.

According to Tan, the distinction between duties of justice and duties of humanity also applies in the domestic context. In some understandings of distributive equality, the difference between justice and humanity is a moot one except when there is a disagreement over whether or not there really are any duties of justice, in which case those who answer in the affirmative and advocate distributive equality appear more radical than those who answer in the negative. On a luck egalitarian understanding of equality, however, the distinction gains significance even in the absence of disagreement. According to Tan, duties of justice begin at the point where duties of humanity end, and end at the point where duties of humanity begin. This entails, in part, that the duty to redistribute to those who are less well-off but who lie above the appropriate sufficiency threshold is a duty of justice and not also a duty of humanity. More interestingly, it also entails that the duty to redistribute to those who are less well-off and who lie below the sufficiency threshold is a duty of humanity and not also a duty of justice. This way of understanding the distinction between egalitarian justice and humanitarian aid offers luck egalitarians a way around the harshness objection. Just as there is no duty of justice to aid the less well-off who fall below the sufficiency threshold, so too there is no duty of justice to refrain from providing aid in cases where a person's need is traceable to her imprudence. Duties of humanity and justice occupy different domains and thus there is no space in which luck egalitarianism could require the excessive harshness Anderson and Scheffler contemplate.[66]

Dworkin's strategy for dealing with the harshness objection relies on his hypothetical insurance device.[67] He claims that the effects of any particular form of bad luck on the holdings of the disadvantaged are justifiably compensable insofar as a rational citizen would have hypothetically insured against it. As one might expect, considerations such as the likelihood of being afflicted by a particular form of bad luck, the severity of the consequences associated with it, and the cost of compensating the victims of said consequences all factor into determining whether and the extent to which a person who suffers bad luck is to be compensated. According to Dworkin, however, his insurance market device covers more than just bad *brute* luck. It also covers bad *option* luck in cases where it would be rational to insure against it. To be sure, those cases will be fewer, as the problem of moral hazard would make the premiums associated with insuring against option luck higher on average than those associated with insuring against brute luck. Still, insuring against option luck would arguably be rational at times, especially where it threatens one's basic needs. For example, he maintains that a society seeking to redistribute in accordance with his insurance scheme would compensate for prolonged unemployment and extremely low income. These causes of poverty will in some cases be unrelated to choice, such as unemployment caused by a genetically produced lack of marketable talent, but in other cases it will be due to bad decisions about education, training, investment, and so on. According to Dworkin, his insurance market would not fail to compensate the unemployed or low income earners in cases where their poverty is choice related.[68] Compensation for unemployment would to some extent be contingent upon willingness to work when work becomes available,[69] but unemployment (and low income) caused by poor decisions is presumably common enough, and its effects severe enough, to make paying the requisite insurance premium rational.

Do the defenses of luck egalitarianism offered by Tan and Dworkin make a defeasible luck egalitarian principle theoretically unnecessary? Perhaps we can dispense with defeasible luck equality in favor of a suitably qualified luck egalitarian position that is both defendable and capable of playing an action-guiding role in politics?

Beginning with Dworkin, despite having an explicit reply to the harshness objection, he is nonetheless still vulnerable to it. As Tan himself points out, it is not clear that the hypothetical insurance device can justify securing basic needs against bad option luck across the board. Though it is likely rational for hypothetical insurance buyers to insure against the possibility that future imprudence might, at some point, endanger the satisfaction of their basic needs, Tan is right to say that an insurance policy that protects basic needs without any stipulations about disqualifying behavior would have extremely high premiums. A person who must be repeatedly bailed out is much more expensive to society than a person who must only be bailed once or twice in her otherwise prudent life. However, guaranteeing basic needs across the board requires protecting the former person as much as it requires protecting the latter person. As a result, it may not be rational for a hypothetical insurance buyer to fully protect her basic needs against the possibility of bad option luck. Thus Dworkin's theory remains vulnerable to the harshness objection.[70]

Suppose we were to grant that Tan's and Dworkin's replies to the harshness objection succeed. Even if we were to do so, it is questionable whether their versions of luck egalitarianism cohere sufficiently with our all-things-considered judgments of right and wrong.[71] Rejecting defeasibility deprives them of a resource with which to reply to other objections as well, such as Wolff's above-discussed worry about respect. Unless luck equality is defeasible, a balance between it and the requirements of respect cannot be struck.

Consider also the famous levelling down problem. According to this objection, it is an absurd implication of distributive egalitarianism that an equal state of affairs is to be preferred over an unequal state of affairs in which some are better off than they would be under equality but none are worse off.[72] In fact, it could also be objected that the distributive egalitarian must prefer an equal state of affairs over an unequal state of affairs in which *everyone* is better off than they would be under equality.[73] For luck egalitarians that see luck equality as a defeasible value, a straightforward reply is available. They can claim that levelling down for the sake of equality is good in one respect and yet nonetheless wrong, all things considered. Just as luck equality must leave space for values like compassion and respect, it must also leave space for efficiency.[74] For egalitarians like Dworkin and Tan, however, the matter is more complicated. According to Michael Otsuka, Dworkin's commitment to equality as the 'sovereign virtue' deprives him of the conceptual resources needed to respond to the levelling-down problem,[75] and the same objection might very well be made against Tan. Of course, Otsuka may be wrong. Other replies to the levelling-down problem are available.[76] My point is merely that rejecting defeasibility leaves luck egalitarians more vulnerable here.

Rather than rehash arguments from the literature on levelling down, I would like to focus on an issue that is separate from whether indefeasible versions of luck egalitarianism are adequate guides to political action. More specifically, in their efforts to maintain a tight connection with action guidance, Tan and Dworkin render their theories incapable of recognizing some pretty clear cases of unfairness. This is not a bad thing per se. However, it does entail that the evaluative capacity of their theories is lacking.

Let's consider Tan first. As we have noted, Tan avoids the harshness objection by limiting the scope of luck egalitarianism to inequalities that lie above the sufficiency threshold. In his view, our duties to those who fall below the sufficiency threshold are not duties of justice, but rather duties of humanity. It follows from this, he claims, that a correct understanding of luck egalitarianism does not require harsh treatment of the imprudent in cases where basic needs are at stake. Since it is humanity (compassion), not justice, that gives us reason to redistribute to those in absolute poverty, justice also cannot be a reason to withhold distribution in cases where a person is responsible for her own poverty. Justice and humanity occupy different domains, he thinks. Humanity covers absolute poverty, that is, deprivation that falls below the sufficiency threshold, and justice covers inequalities that lie above that threshold.[77] In fact, Tan explicitly rejects the view that either compassion or another value 'trumps' justice in cases where absolute poverty is traceable to imprudence; thus he explicitly rejects the claim that justice applies, even in a defeasible manner, below the sufficiency threshold. According to him, accepting defeasibility in order to reply to the harshness objection is a Pyrrhic victory (a claim I challenge in the next section).[78]

Though the global justice literature's distinction between duties of justice and duties of humanity affords Tan a convenient reply to the harshness objection, it doesn't take much reflection to realize that considerations of fairness extend beyond the boundaries he sets. Consider a hypothetical society whose members all fall below the sufficiency threshold. Since no one in this society is able to fully meet all of her basic needs, everyone is poorly-off in absolute terms. Still, some of the members of this society are better off than others. Let's say that the members of one group are unable to fully meet most of their basic needs and thus tend to die at quite a young age. The members of another group, in contrast, are able to meet most of their basic needs most of the time but regularly suffer from malnutrition because they do not have adequate access to food. This latter group still leads what we would consider to be a very hard life in absolute terms, but it is considerably better off than the former group. Granted that the inequality between these groups is not traceable to choice, are we to refrain from judging it to be a case of unfairness simply because it occurs below the sufficiency threshold? Presumably not. Of course, we might be willing to grant that in circumstances of such dire need, other concerns take precedence over fairness, all things considered. For instance, it might be more important to increase the number of people who achieve sufficiency than it is to eliminate inequalities between those below the sufficiency threshold. That does not somehow remove the unfairness, though. It just makes it comparatively less pressing.

Let's consider a more conventional example. Consider inequalities of the kind egalitarians frequently address, namely inequalities between those who are quite poorly off through no fault of their own in both relative and absolute terms and those whose social and/or genetic luck have made them quite well-off in both relative and absolute terms. By Tan's account, the duties owed by the well-off to the poorly-off in this case are, at least at first, strictly duties of humanity. It is only after the poorly-off have been raised above the sufficiency threshold that the duties owed to them become duties of justice. As with the previous case, though, there is an unfairness not captured by Tan's analysis. In particular, his theory does not account for the judgment that the inequality between those who are well-off and those who are in absolute poverty is unfair. Why is recognizing this unfairness important? It is important because egalitarians would otherwise be unable to say a lot of things we want to be able to say. For example, we would be unable to say that the inequality between rich group X and poor group Y is *less unfair* once poor group Y has been raised above the sufficiency threshold. In other words, we would be unable to say that our initial redistributive efforts have mitigated the unfairness between them. What's more, though we would be able to say that the inequality between rich group X and comparatively but not absolutely poor group Y is unfair, we would (absurdly) not be able to say that the inequality between rich group X and comparatively even poorer plus absolutely poor group Z is unfair. Since we want to be able to say these things, however, we must also admit that Tan's luck egalitarianism lacks the capacity to identify certain cases of distributive unfairness.

The above cases suggest two things about defeasible luck equality. The first is that, for evaluative purposes, it cannot be ignored. Even if Tan's version of luck egalitarianism can adequately specify our all-things-considered distributive duties, it cannot account for all the instances where we want to deem an inequality to be unfair. As such, and at the very least, defeasible luck equality should be preserved alongside Tan's action guiding luck egalitarianism for the purpose of filling in the evaluative gaps his theory leaves behind.

Second, the above cases, specifically the more conventional ones, also suggest that ignoring defeasible luck equality can lead to a mischaracterization of our all-things-considered duties. As I noted above, the unchosen inequality between the well-off and those below the sufficiency threshold should be recognized as unfair. This is important for evaluative clarity about the status of that inequality, but it is also important to how we understand the relevant duty. Once we recognize that the inequality is unfair, the all-things-considered duty to aid the poorly-off becomes more than just a duty grounded in humanity or compassion: it becomes a duty grounded by fairness too. Unlike the cases highlighted by the harshness critique, where fairness and compassion clash, cases where the poorly-off are unable to meet basic needs through no fault of their own are cases where reasons of fairness and compassion overlap, providing mutual support for the conclusion that the needy should receive aid. This produces a significant difference between the kinds of all-things-considered duties we can owe to those below the sufficiency threshold. Some of our all-things-considered duties are solely duties of humanity because fairness prohibits redistribution but is trumped by compassion. Other duties, however, are all-things-considered duties of fairness and humanity because fairness counts alongside compassion as one of the reasons justifying redistribution.

It is important to note that accurately classifying our duties to those below the sufficiency threshold is not merely a matter of nomenclature. Recognizing that some of our duties to those below the sufficiency threshold are duties of humanity but not fairness, while others are duties of humanity and fairness, should matter when ranking our distributive priorities in the real world. Ceteris paribus, when scarce resources leave one faced with a choice between helping either the imprudent needy or those who are needy through no fault of their own, the latter should take precedence. Characterizing all our duties to those below the sufficiency threshold as solely duties of humanity thus deprives us of important, normatively relevant information.

Predictably, Dworkin's hypothetical insurance device, like Tan's version of luck equality, also excludes various cases of unfairness. For example, consider a hypothetical set of people who are the same in all relevant respects except that one member of the set is worse off because she has been seriously disadvantaged by bad brute luck. We can expect that Dworkin's insurance scheme would compensate the disadvantaged member, thus recognizing the unfairness of the inequality between her and the other members. However, one of the functions of Dworkin's insurance scheme is to set a limit on the amount of compensation owed to any victim of brute luck.[79] The disadvantaged are entitled to compensation, but only insofar as they would hypothetically have insured against whatever befell them. As a result, according to his theory, the victims of bad brute luck are not always entitled to *full* compensation, that is, to compensation that is sufficient to place them at the same level as their luckier co-citizens.[80] The upshot is that Dworkin's theory, like Tan's, has limited evaluative capacity. In order to capture the unfairness of residual inequalities, defeasible luck equality must fill in the evaluative gap.

Is the above analysis fair to Dworkin, though? Does Dworkin's theory really neglect residual inequalities? While it is clear in Tan's case that defeasible luck equality is being neglected in favor of an action-guiding version of it, it is less obvious that this is the case with Dworkin. In fact, an appreciation for the manner in which he derives his insurance device suggests that he would perhaps agree that something like defeasible luck equality is indispensable. According to Dworkin, it is theoretically desirable for a distribution to be "ambition-sensitive" but not "endowment-sensitive."[81] However, he thinks that various practical problems make it both infeasible and undesirable to attempt to fully realize such a distribution in the real world. Practical problems he discusses include our inability to discern which part of a person's talents is traceable to choice and which part to genetics,[82] as well the inefficiency of attempting to provide full compensation for bad luck in cases where doing so is expensive and unlikely to be effective (e.g., severe spinal cord injuries).[83] To deal with such difficulties, Dworkin recommends that his hypothetical insurance device be used to guide political practice instead.

From the above description, it does not seem unreasonable to conclude that Dworkin is employing a distinction very much akin to the distinction between a principle that serves as a conception of a fundamental value and a principle that serves as a guide to action. The ideal of an ambition-sensitive but endowment-insensitive distribution, though unsuitable for purposes of guiding political practice, is nonetheless used to justify that which is suitable for guiding political practice, namely the hypothetical insurance device. After all, his hypothetical insurance device still makes room for brute luck to be compensated. It just places limitations on compensation in deference to the fact that the resources available to a society are finite. What's more, there is a sense (albeit an attenuated sense) in which cases of bad brute luck that the state refuses to compensate are in effect converted into cases of bad option luck. Under institutions designed to emulate a hypothetical insurance market, the state only refuses to compensate cases of bad brute luck that would be hypothetically irrational to insure against. Thus when a citizen is denied compensation for a disadvantage traceable to her circumstances, it is only because she would have hypothetically *chosen* not to buy coverage.[84] As a result, the hypothetical insurance device can justify withholding compensation on the basis of reasoning that is akin to, and in fact modeled after, justifications for disadvantage that invoke responsibility for choice as the basis for non-intervention. Given all of this, it is not unreasonable to interpret the ideal of an ambition-sensitive, endowment-insensitive distribution as Dworkin's fundamental, defeasible principle of luck egalitarian fairness, and his insurance market device, in turn, as his conception of all-things-considered institutional rightness.

Were the above understanding Dworkin's own understanding of his theory, there would be little question about the place of defeasible luck equality within it. Interestingly, however, this is not how he understands his work. According to Dworkin, the hypothetical insurance market is not a pragmatic compromise. Though it is indeed responsive to facts about the real world, it nonetheless fully represents justice, rather than an imperfectly fair (and thus imperfectly just) compromise between fairness and other considerations. In other words, Dworkin's insurance market is supposed to be both a theory of what distributive justice *is* and a theory of what is politically required of us with respect to distribution, all things considered. The two are not supposed to come apart. Why? Because the insurance market device is just as much an interpretation of abstract equality, that is, equal consideration, as the ideal of luck equality is. According to Dworkin, for a theory to be a compelling interpretation of abstract equality is sufficient for it to be a theory of full, uncompromised justice.[85] If he is right, then pure luck equality is more of a heuristic device in the context of his theory than anything else. As the correct conception of equal consideration for idealized circumstances, luck equality can be used to help us discern what equal consideration requires of us in real-world circumstances, but luck equality is not itself the 'sovereign virtue.' Rather, equal consideration is, and it can be adapted to the circumstances we face in the real world by formulating an interpretation more practicable than the principle of luck equality, namely the hypothetical insurance market (though, of course, there is still some distance between the insurance market and political practice insofar as a tax scheme cannot model it perfectly).

The relationship between equal consideration, a conception of distributive fairness, and a conception of all-things-considered institutional rightness is a complex and important one. In fact, this relationship will be one of the topics discussed in Chapter 5. Since I will be dealing with it at length later, I will not discuss it too much here. I will say, however, that we should understand both (a) the motivation to retain a close connection between luck egalitarianism and action guidance, and (b) the related claim that a practicable interpretation of equal consideration (the hypothetical insurance device) is a full, uncompromised theory of justice; in relation to (c) the idea of *primacy*. As Rawls puts it: "Justice is the first virtue of social institutions, as truth is of systems of thought. A theory however elegant and economical must be rejected or revised if it is untrue; likewise laws and institutions no matter how efficient and well-arranged must be reformed or abolished if they are unjust."[86] This statement is sometimes associated with Rawls's focus on institutional justice, but its force goes beyond what justice applies to. It's also a statement about the supreme importance of justice relative to other virtues. It states that a society's institutions, regardless of the other virtues they might exhibit, must conform to the virtue of justice in order to be acceptable. For anyone who takes this idea seriously, it might be thought that an important element of any plausible theory of justice is that its principles be indefeasible.[87] A conception of justice that subjects itself to trade-offs (e.g., trade-offs with efficiency) can at best be said to have delivered the content of *a* virtue of social institutions, not *the first* virtue of social institutions.

But what should take precedence when articulating a conception of justice: the requirement that a conception of justice cohere with our full range of intuitive judgments about fairness and unfairness, or the requirement that it have primacy? As things stand, these two features of the concept of (narrow) justice, *fairness* and *primacy*, appear to be in dramatic tension with each other. A principle that coheres with our full range of intuitive judgments of fairness can supply necessary and sufficient conditions for the fairness of a distribution, thus meeting the fairness requirement, but it will also thereby become vulnerable to counter-examples that make trade-offs necessary (e.g., the counter-examples in the harshness critique). In contrast, a principle that is normatively robust enough to serve an indefeasible, action-guiding role can satisfy the primacy requirement, but it must also put aside certain judgments of fairness in doing so (e.g., the judgment that it is unfair to compensate the imprudent needy). Is it the case then that any principle satisfying the fairness requirement lacks primacy, and that any principle satisfying the primacy requirement is imperfectly fair? The answer to this question will have to wait until Chapter 5.

5. The Practical Significance of Defeasible Luck Equality

In the previous section, I hope to have demonstrated that a defeasible luck egalitarian principle is indispensable. Even if Tan's and Dworkin's theories escape the criticisms that challenge their capacity for action guidance (and it's questionable whether they do), only a defeasible version of luck egalitarianism is capable of cohering with all our intuitive judgments of fairness in distribution.

Though my reader may agree that I have accomplished my goal, she might nonetheless reasonably wonder what we are left with at this point. Sure, luck egalitarianism is a compelling conception of a defeasible value. And sure, it supplies us with a useful evaluative criterion, one that captures intuitive cases of fairness and unfairness even in instances where the fairness of an inequality is not sufficient reason to leave it intact or where the unfairness of an inequality is not sufficient reason to eliminate it. But what's the practical value of such a criterion? Can it contribute anything to normative deliberation?

The above question can be answered in part with reference to our discussion about recognizing considerations of fairness below the sufficiency threshold. Though it is true under normal circumstances that both the prudent needy and the imprudent needy should be assisted, it is nonetheless practically significant to recognize that fairness supports compensating the former but not the latter. Why? Because our circumstances are not always normal, and reasons that are typically defeated can become effective when the relevant facts change. With respect to assisting the needy in particular, an important circumstantial factor is the availability of resources with which to provide assistance. When resources are sufficient to assist both the prudent and the imprudent, recognizing the unfairness of assisting the latter does nothing to affect our course of action. When resources are no longer sufficient, however, recognizing that we have reasons of humanity and fairness to assist the prudent needy but only reasons of humanity to assist the imprudent needy becomes practically important. Ceteris paribus, if it isn't feasible to assist both the prudent and the imprudent, then the prudent should take precedence.

For example, suppose that two cities located in the same region or province have been having an unusually large frequency of power outages. We will call them city A and city B. The outages are sometimes quite long, and the residents of both cities have had to endure severe difficulties in equal proportions, such as food spoilage, traffic problems, lack of heat during cold weather, and so forth. After investigating the problem, the government decides that the most effective course of action it can take over the next five years is to build an additional power plant. Unfortunately, it turns out that the plant will not suffice to completely solve both cities' power problems. There are only a limited number of areas where the plant can be safely constructed, and while some of these areas would afford either city sufficient access to resolve its power problems, none would afford both cities sufficient access. Furthermore, let us suppose that access cannot be divided evenly. No matter the choice made, either city A or city B will have superior access to the power generated by the new plant.

When making a decision about where to build the plant, it matters whether the residents of cities A and B are differentially responsible for their situation. If the power outages in city A are primarily due to the stress its residents' excessive power consumption places on the local power grid, whereas the outages in city B are primarily due to circumstances beyond its residents' control, then shouldn't city B be given better access to the additional power? Residents in both cities are having their basic needs threatened by the outages, but only the residents in city B have a claim grounded in fairness. This difference between them matters under the circumstances.

Interestingly, Tan thinks that his version of luck egalitarianism is capable of consistently prioritizing the prudent needy over the imprudent needy in circumstances of scarcity. He writes:

> What my account can accept is that the maker of a bad choice in this case will unfortunately not get what she is in fact entitled to as a matter of humanitarian principle because of other considerations (such as abject scarcity), that her claim is overridden by the claim of another. This does not mean that she is no longer as a matter of principle entitled to assistance; she remains entitled and this entitlement is not invalidated. It is just that, under the circumstance, it is possible that her principled claim is overridden by other considerations. . . . Choice can be a tie-breaker even in the domain of basic needs in tragic situations *without* implying the premise that a person who has made a bad choice forfeits all claim to assistance.[88]

In the above quote, Tan correctly notes that choice can function as a tie breaker between the claims of those below the sufficiency threshold without thereby implying that the imprudent needy have no claim to assistance. What he does not seem to realize, though, is that by making this move he sacrifices the indefeasibility of his principle. As we have already noted, one way of replying to the harshness objection is to claim that luck equality is trumped by one or more other values when the basic needs of the imprudent are at stake. The novelty of Tan's reply is that it avoids conceding that luck equality is sometimes defeated by other values. Since, in his view, egalitarian justice only applies to inequalities above the sufficiency threshold, luck equality never comes into conflict with the values that uphold basic needs. Unfortunately, Tan cannot consistently maintain that luck equality never conflicts with upholding basic needs *and* that it functions as a tie breaker between the prudent needy and the imprudent needy in circumstances where it is not feasible to assist both. Conceding that luck equality functions as a tie breaker below the sufficiency threshold presupposes that it applies below the sufficiency threshold. And if luck equality applies below the sufficiency, then there is no longer any principled basis for Tan's claim that it is not trumped by competing values under circumstances where it is feasible to assist both the prudent needy and imprudent needy.

The practical significance of defeasible luck equality will become further apparent via an analysis of its relationship with Rawls's difference principle. Though it has been argued with some plausibility that Rawls's theory does not even implicitly rely upon luck egalitarianism,[89] it must be admitted that the difference principle has a lot going for it from a luck egalitarian perspective.

First, the difference principle is responsive to the fact that one cannot be held responsible for the social group into which one is born, as it requires that the distribution of opportunities between individuals with different group membership but the same talents and ambitions be equal. Second, it recognizes that natural talents are largely the product of genetic luck and thus that there are reasons of fairness to limit the extent of their distributive influence. Third, though the difference principle permits some inequality between the talented and the untalented, Rawls qualifies this with a caveat. The justifiability of inequalities consistent with the difference principle is contingent upon it being the case that those inequalities not be too great. If it turned out that the realization of equal liberty and fair equality of opportunity were not enough to limit the size of inequalities necessary to improve the position of the worst-off, then the difference principle would not be justified.[90] In sum, the difference principle's commitment to fair equality of opportunity and the mitigation of genetic luck's distributive impact, combined with the justificatory assumption that inequalities will be limited in size, makes it a pretty reasonable regulatory principle from the perspective of defeasible luck equality.

It should also be noted that the difference principle compares favorably to action-guiding versions of luck egalitarianism when considered in light of the criticisms the latter must struggle with. For one, the difference principle avoids the levelling-down problem, as it permits inequalities necessary to improve the position of the worst-off. What's more, it straightforwardly avoids the harshness objection, as all members of the worst-off group are the beneficiaries of compensation, regardless of whether they are prudent or imprudent.

As I will now proceed to argue, however, defeasible luck equality sees the difference principle's regulatory optimality as temporary. When factual constraints that limit the extent to which luck equality can be implemented on its own or in unison with other values are lifted, modifications to the difference principle are subsequently needed in order to restore its all-things-considered optimality. Pablo Gilabert's work is helpful for understanding this point. He notes that an appreciation for the malleability of *soft* feasibility constraints requires that we take a 'transitional standpoint.'[91] The main implication of his work for defeasible luck equality is that its implementation is not simply a matter of adopting action-guiding principles that reflect feasibility constraints and the requirements of other defeasible principles. It also requires paying attention to the ways in which our actions can affect our social and political context, and thus the ways in which they can affect the feasibility of realizing more desirable states of affairs in the future.[92] For example, Wolff's concern about disproportionate scrutiny and distrust is a problem with respect to which taking a transitional standpoint makes sense. As we noted, Wolff worries that in a highly unequal society, the implementation of luck egalitarianism will reasonably be experienced as distrustful and disrespectful by poorly-off social groups, as the conditionality of luck egalitarian compensation would require that they be subject to a disproportionately large amount of scrutiny. However, the situation is different in a society where group membership does not affect one's opportunities and thus where no particular set of social or racial groups bears the lion's share of society's burdens. Implementing luck equality in such a society would not require disproportionate scrutiny. The upshot of this observation is to take a transitional standpoint with respect to the implementation of luck equality in a highly unequal society. Since the pursuit of unconditional redistribution promises to yield a context where the facts do not force a conflict between fairness and respect, unconditional redistribution should be pursued until conditional redistribution becomes more reasonable.

Getting back to the difference principle, the above discussion of disproportionate scrutiny suggests one area where that principle's optimality is temporary. Though considerations of humanity/compassion require securing a basic-needs floor, below which the poorly-off should not be permitted to fall (except in situations like the power outage scenario), distinguishing between the prudent and the imprudent above this point is reasonable so long as it does not require imposing disproportionate scrutiny. This suggests that the difference principle is only initially optimal. Once fair equality of opportunity has eliminated inequalities of opportunity traceable to group membership, disproportionate scrutiny will no longer be needed to distinguish between the prudent and the imprudent. In such circumstances, I suggest that instead of ensuring that inequalities maximally benefit the least well-off in general, it is more appropriate to combine (a) a basic-needs floor that covers the imprudent needy with (b) a commitment to ensuring that inequalities between the well-off and the poorly-off maximally benefit those who are poorly off through no fault of their own. The upshot would be a society where the imprudent have their basic needs met but, out of recognition for the unfairness of assisting them, do not receive maximal benefit. The victims of bad brute luck, in contrast, receive maximal benefit, and are thus better off than the imprudent. However, a certain amount of inequality between those with poor brute luck and the talented well-off is permitted, when necessary, out of deference to efficiency and the importance of avoiding the levelling-down problem. From the perspective of defeasible luck equality, this strikes me as the best institutional regulatory route.[93]

As we will soon see, the tension between fairness and efficiency associated with the need to offer incentives is, like the tension between fairness and respect, contingent. Whereas the tension between fairness and respect is contingent upon the *fact* of existing social inequalities, the tension between fairness and efficiency is contingent upon the *fact* that the talented are not motivated to be equally productive under a fully egalitarian tax regime. Further discussion of the matter will have to wait until Chapter 4; however, as it is there where I address Cohen's work on incentives and the scope of justice.

6. Conclusion

This chapter has argued that there are important benefits to understanding luck egalitarianism as a conception of a defeasible value. Though an increased resilience to criticism is certainly one of those benefits, defeasibility makes it possible for luck egalitarianism to cohere with the full range of intuitive judgments of fairness, both those that coincide with all-things-considered rightness and those that come apart from it. This observation is theoretically significant, since a principle that does not cohere with our less normatively robust judgments of fairness cannot provide a necessary and sufficient criterion for distributive fairness; that is, it cannot capture the *essence* of fairness. As we saw, it is also practically significant, since ignoring judgments that come apart from rightness makes it impossible to accurately categorize our duties, thereby depriving us of the normative information needed to rank them.

Perhaps the most important function of defeasible luck equality is that it can be used to evaluate the extent to which our all-things-considered principles fall short of perfect fairness. Such an evaluation may be of limited use in the present, but it could be more helpful in the future, as all-things-considered optimality is a contingent property. In particular, Rawls's version of the difference principle is fine for now, but a more choice-sensitive version of it will be preferable once fair equality of opportunity has succeeded at eliminating the danger of disproportionate scrutiny. So long as scrutiny is not disproportionately focused on particular social or racial groups and interviewers are sufficiently sensitive to ward off 'shameful revelation,' it will be possible to distinguish between prudent and imprudent members of the worst-off class without jeopardizing respect.

Notes

1. Cohen (1989) p. 933.
2. See Wolff (1998); Anderson (1999) pp. 295–300; Scheffler (2003) p. 33; and Scheffler (2005) p. 15.
3. See, for example, Brown (2005); Barry (2006); Casal (2007) pp. 321–3; Segall (2007); and Cohen (2009) pp. 34–6.
4. Tan (2008) p. 679, footnote 25; and Tan (2012) pp. 125–6.
5. See Kymlicka (2002) pp. 75–9; and Kymlicka (2006) pp. 17–8.
6. See Wolff (1998); Anderson (1999) pp. 295–300; Scheffler (2003) p. 33; and Scheffler (2005) p. 15.
7. See Dworkin (2002) pp. 113–4; Tan (2008) pp. 669–71 and pp. 675–9; and Tan (2012) pp. 100–2 and pp. 119–26.
8. See Anderson (1999) pp. 287–337.
9. See Dworkin (2000) p. 89; Arneson (1989) p. 86;and Cohen (1989) p. 916. See also endnote 7 in Chapter 1 of this volume.
10. Dworkin (2000) pp. 73–83. For some recent literature questioning the idea that inequalities produced by option luck are, from a luck egalitarian standpoint, entirely just, see Barry (2008) and Cohen (2011).
11. The first of these views is Dworkin's, the second Arneson's, and the third Cohen's. See Dworkin (2000) pp. 79–80; Arneson (1989); and Cohen (1989) pp. 15–9.
12. The following account of luck egalitarianism's advantages over Rawls's theory of justice draws extensively upon the account provided by Will Kymlicka. See his discussion in Chapter 3 of Kymlicka (2002).
13. Rawls (1971) p. 74.
14. Kymlicka (2002) pp. 70–2. For similar comments, see Dworkin (2000) p. 113.
15. See Kymlicka (2002) pp. 75–9; and Kymlicka (2006) pp. 17–8.

16. See Scheffler (2003) pp. 17–9; and Scheffler (2005) pp. 10–4.
17. Scheffler (2003) p. 19; and Scheffler (2005) p. 13.
18. Arneson (1989) p. 87; and Cohen (1989) p. 7.
19. Kymlicka (2002) p. 20.
20. Arneson (1989) p. 87.
21. Dworkin (2000) pp. 77–83, pp. 90–2, and pp. 99–109.
22. Wolff (1998) pp. 110–5.
23. Anderson (1999) pp. 304–7.
24. See Scheffler (2003) pp. 32–3; and Scheffler (2005) pp. 15–6.
25. For various examples produced in support of the harshness criticism, see Anderson (1999) pp. 295–300; Scheffler (2003) p. 33; and Scheffler (2005) p. 15.
26. See Anderson (1999) pp. 312–26; Scheffler (2003) pp. 31–9; Scheffler (2005) pp. 17–23; and Hinton (2001) pp. 80–1 and pp. 85–7. Though Anderson and Hinton specifically endorse limiting redistribution to provision of a basic minimum, Scheffler is more open ended. Rather than committing himself to a particular redistributive scheme, he limits himself to specifying that whatever form of redistribution egalitarians endorse will have to be justified with reference to its instrumental significance for the creation and maintenance of egalitarian social relations.
27. See, for example, Cohen (2008) p. 271 and pp. 300–2; Anderson (2010) esp. pp. 17–22; and Tomlin (2012).
28. Scanlon (2006) pp. 85–7. For Cohen's explicit endorsement of Scanlon's description, see Cohen (2008) p. 302, footnote 35.
29. See Cohen (2008) Chapter 7.
30. Cohen (2008) pp. 3–6.
31. Cohen (2008) p. 268 and pp. 306–7. For discussions of the distinction between evaluative claims and normative claims, see Lawford-Smith (2010) pp. 357–61; Gilabert (2011) pp. 55–9; Tomlin (2012) pp. 377–8 and pp. 383–5; and Valentini (2012) pp. 657–8.
32. Cohen (2009) pp. 56–7.
33. Arneson (1989) p. 81.
34. See Brown (2005); Barry (2006); Casal (2007) pp. 321–3; and Segall (2007).
35. Scheffler (2003) p. 33.
36. One way a luck egalitarian might reply to Scheffler, at least with respect to his discussion of differential professional success, is by arguing that the point of distributive justice, and thus of luck equality, is is to provide the fair background conditions needed to pursue a meaningful life. On this understanding of the function (or rather one of the functions) of justice, luck egalitarianism's role is to specify the institutional conditions that must be in place for the distributive inequalities that emerge between citizens as a result of choices and transactions over time to be just (see Rawls 2001 pp. 52–4). From this, it seems to follow that luck egalitarianism is consistent with differentially rewarding members of the same profession, as one's profession (at least in many cases) is only meaningful if there is some way of recognizing the extent of one's contribution.

    The reason I have chosen not to employ this reply is because the idea that justice is about setting background conditions for the pursuit of a meaningful life is a distinctly Rawlsian notion, one bound up with his belief that justice is specifically about setting up the institutional conditions needed to ensure a just distribution of goods across social positions over time, rather than about constantly interfering with liberty in order to continuously preserve a particular distribution across individuals (see Rawls 1971 p. 7; and Nozick 1974 pp. 160–4). Thus while this reply is likely appropriate if one conceives of luck egalitarianism as a theory of institutional rightness, it is not appropriate if, like me, one understands luck egalitarianism as a conception of a defeasible value. The point of luck egalitarianism, on my understanding, is to specify the conditions necessary and sufficient for a distribution to count as fair, and doing so requires achieving coherence with all our intuitive judgments of fairness, including those which aren't normatively robust. As such, defeasible luck equality must be responsive to the intuition that it is unfair when unequal levels of occupational success emerge between members of the same profession who were equally careful about selecting a career suited to their abilities and who devote an equal amount of time and effort to their work. This intuition may very well not suffice to justify withholding recognition of differential levels of contribution, and the reason for its insufficiency may very well be because withholding recognition of differential contribution would deprive many professions of their meaning, but that doesn't mean we should refrain from evaluating such cases as unfair. Though defeasible luck equality is certainly connected to the background conditions needed to pursue a meaningful life, its role is not to set those conditions, but rather to partially justify the action-guiding institutional principles that do.

37. See Cohen's discussion of 'community' in Cohen (2009) pp. 34–45; and Shlomi Segall's discussion of 'solidarity' in Segall (2007) pp. 195–8.
38. Anderson (1999) pp. 300–1.
39. Carl Knight also suggests that luck egalitarians could employ fairness rather than paternalism to ground mandatory participation, though he does not explicitly realize that this is only possible if fairness is defeasible. See Knight (2005) pp. 62–3.
40. For influential internalist views, see Frankfurt (1971); and Watson (1989). For accounts emphasizing the importance of incorporating external conditions, see G. Dworkin (1976); Christman (1991); and Christman (2007).
41. In a number of passages, Scheffler suggests that he finds luck equality much more plausible when treated as an ingredient in a distributive scheme instead of the sole principle. See Schefller (2005) p. 22 and p. 24.
42. Anderson (1999) p. 305.
43. Anderson (1999) p. 306.
44. For thoughts similar to those I express here, see Carl Knight (2005) pp. 64–5.
45. See Tan (2008) p. 665 and p. 667. See also Chapter 2's discussion of the relationship between distributive fairness and the value of a good.
46. Wolff (1998) pp. 120–1; and Wolff (2010) p. 346.
47. Wolff (1998) pp. 98–103; and Wolff (2010) pp. 340–3.
48. Wolff (2010) p. 345 and pp. 347–8.
49. Wolff (1998) pp. 110–3.
50. See my discussion of luck egalitarianism and paternalism above.
51. See Anderson (1999) pp. 312–5; Scheffler (2003) pp. 21–4 and pp. 31–9; and Scheffler (2005) pp. 17–23.
52. Anderson (1999) p. 313.
53. See Scheffler's description of the consequences of social inequality in Scheffler (2005) p. 19.
54. Rawls (1971) p. 440.
55. Rawls (1971) p. 440.
56. Rawls (2001) p. 59.
57. Scheffler (2005) p. 19. For work that defends flourishing as the appropriate egalitarian metric, see Sypnowich (2003); and Sypnowich (2014).
58. Kymlicka (2006) p. 27.
59. Cohen (2009) pp. 34–5.
60. Cohen (2009) pp. 34–6.
61. Scheffler (2005) p. 19.
62. Cohen (2008) Chapter 1 and Chapter 3.
63. See Dworkin (2002); Dworkin (2003); and Tan (2008).
64. See, for example, Rawls (1999) pp. 113–5; and Nagel (2005) p. 118.

65. For a defense of the claim that sufficiency exhausts our distributive obligations to the disadvantaged, see Frankfurt (1987). For an extensive critique of Frankfurt's position, see Casal (2007).
66. Tan (2008) pp. 669–71 and pp. 675–9; and Tan (2012) pp. 100–2 and pp. 119–26.
67. For discussion of his hypothetical insurance device, see Dworkin (2000) pp. 73–83.
68. Dworkin (2002) pp. 113–4.
69. Dworkin (2000) pp. 334–8.
70. Tan (2008) pp. 678–9.
71. For criticisms of Dworkin's theory, see the articles about his book *Sovereign Virtue* in volume 113, issue 1, of the journal *Ethics*. For a critique of Tan's theory, see Nath (2014).
72. See Partfit (2002) p. 98.
73. See, for example, Christiano (2007) pp. 71–2.
74. See Cohen (2008) pp. 315–23; and Temkin (2002) pp. 154–5.
75. Otsuka (2002) pp. 45–8.
76. For alternative replies to the levelling-down problem, see Dworkin (2002) pp. 122–4; and Christiano (2007) pp. 71–8.
77. Tan (2008) pp. 669–71; and Tan (2012) pp. 100–2.
78. Tan (2008) p. 679, footnote 25; and Tan (2012) pp. 125–6.
79. See Dworkin's discussion of the contrast between his and other approaches to compensating the handicapped in Dworkin (2000) pp. 79–80. See also Kymlicka (2002) pp. 76–7.
80. For similar remarks about Dworkin's hypothetical insurance scheme, see Otsuka (2002) pp. 4
81. Dworkin (2000) p. 89.
82. Dworkin (2000) p. 91.
83. See Dworkin's discussion of healthcare and his rejection of the 'rescue principle' in Dworkin (2000) Chapter 8.
84. Dworkin (2000) pp. 73–7.
85. Dworkin (2002) pp. 120–1; and Dworkin (2003) pp. 190–1.
86. Rawls (1971) p. 3.
87. See Quong (2010) pp. 338–40; and Valentini (2012) p. 658. See also Katherine Eddy's discussion in Eddy (2008) pp. 476–80.
88. Tan (2012) pp. 122–3.
89. See Scheffler (2003) pp. 24–31; and Scheffler (2005) pp. 7–8.
90. Rawls (1971) pp. 157–8.
91. See, for example, Gilabert (2008) pp. 431–8; Gilabert (2011) pp. 59–63; and Gilabert and Lawford-Smith (2012) pp. 821–3.
92. Gilabert (2011) pp. 59–63.
93. For additional discussion of the idea that a regulatory principle's optimality can be temporary, see Johannsen (2016) pp. 182–4.

References

Anderson, Elizabeth. 1999. "What Is the Point of Equality?" *Ethics* 109: 287–337.

Anderson, Elizabeth. 2010. "The Fundamental Disagreement Between Luck Egalitarians and Relational Egalitarians." *Canadian Journal of Philosophy* 40(suppl. 1): 1–23.

Arneson, Richard. 1989. "Equality and Equal Opportunity for Welfare." *Philosophical Studies* 56: 77–93.

Barry, Nicholas. 2006. "Defending Luck Egalitarianism." *Journal of Applied Philosophy* 23: 89–107.

Barry, Nicholas. 2008. "Reassessing Luck Egalitarianism." *The Journal of Politics* 70: 136–50.

Brown, Alexander. 2005. "Luck Egalitarianism and Democratic Equality." *Ethical Perspectives* 12: 293–339.

Casal, Paula. 2007. "Why Sufficiency Is Not Enough." *Ethics* 117: 296–326.

Christiano, Thomas. 2007. "A Foundation for Egalitarianism." In *Egalitarianism: New Essays on the Nature and Value of Equality*. Eds. Nils Holtug and Kasper Lippert-Rasmussen (New York: Clarendon Press).

Christman, John. 1991. "Autonomy and Personal History." *Canadian Journal of Philosophy* 21: 1–24.

Christman, John. 2007. "Autonomy, History, and the Subject of Justice." *Social Theory and Practice* 33: 1–26.

Cohen, G.A. 1989. "On the Currency of Egalitarian Justice." *Ethics* 99: 906–44.

Cohen, G.A. 2008. *Rescuing Justice and Equality* (Cambridge, MA: Harvard University Press).

Cohen, G.A. 2009. *Why Not Socialism?* (Princeton: Princeton University Press).

Cohen, G.A. 2011. "Fairness and Legitimacy in Justice, and: Does Option Luck Ever Preserve Justice?" In *On the Currency of Egalitarian Justice, and Other Essays in Political Philosophy*. Ed. Michael Otsuka (Princeton: Princeton University Press). Pp. 124–43.

Dworkin, Gerald. 1976. "Autonomy and Behavior Control." *Hastings Center Report* 6: 23–8.

Dworkin, Ronald. 2000. *Sovereign Virtue*: *The Theory and Practice of Equality* (Cambridge, MA: Harvard University Press).

Dworkin, Ronald. 2002. "*Sovereign Virtue* Revisited." *Ethics* 113: 106–43.

Dworkin, Ronald. 2003. "Equality, Luck and Hierarchy." *Philosophy and Public Affairs* 31: 190–8.

Eddy, Katherine. 2008. "Against Ideal Right." *Social Theory and Practice* 34: 463–81.

Frankfurt, Harry G. 1971. "Freedom of the Will and the Concept of a Person." *The Journal of Philosophy* 68: 5–20.

Frankfurt, Harry G. 1987. "Equality as a Moral Ideal." *Ethics* 98: 21–43.

Gilabert, Pablo. 2008. "Global Justice and Poverty Relief in Nonideal Circumstances." *Social Theory and Practice* 34: 411–38.

Gilabert, Pablo. 2011. "Debate: Feasibility and Socialism." *The Journal of Political Philosophy* 19: 52–63.

Gilabert, Pablo and Holly Lawford-Smith. 2012. "Political Feasibility: A Conceptual Exploration." *Political Studies* 60: 809–25.

Hinton, Timothy. 2001. "Must Egalitarians Choose Between Fairness and Respect?" *Philosophy and Public Affairs* 30: 72–87.

Johannsen, Kyle. 2016. "Explanation and Justification: Understanding the Functions of Fact-Insensitive Principles." *Socialist Studies* 11(1): 174–86.

Knight, Carl. 2005. "In Defense of Luck Egalitarianism." *Res Publica* 11: 55–73.

Kymlicka, Will. 2002. *Contemporary Political Philosophy: An Introduction* (New York: Oxford University Press).

Kymlicka, Will. 2006. "Left-Liberalism Revisited." In *The Egalitarian Conscience: Essays in Honor of G.A. Cohen*. Ed. Christine Sypnowich (New York: Oxford University Press). Pp. 9–35.

Lawford-Smith, Holly. 2010. "Debate: Ideal Theory—A Reply to Valentini." *The Journal of Political Philosophy* 18: 357–68.

Nagel, Thomas. 2005. "The Problem of Global Justice." *Philosophy and Public Affairs* 33: 113–47.

Nath, Rekha. 2014. "Against Institutional Luck Egalitarianism." *Journal of Ethics & Social Philosophy* 8: 1–19.

Nozick, Robert. 1974. *Anarchy, State, and Utopia* (New York: Basic Books).

Otsuka, Michael. 2002. "Luck, Insurance, and Equality." *Ethics* 113: 40–54.

Parfit, Derek. 2002. "Equality or Priority?" In *The Ideal of Equality*. Eds. Matthew Clayton and Andrew Williams (New York: Palgrave-Macmillan). Pp. 81–125.

Quong, Jonathan. 2010. "Justice Beyond Equality." *Social Theory and Practice* 36: 315–40.

Rawls, John. 1971. *A Theory of Justice* (Cambridge, MA: Belknap Press).

Rawls, John. 1999. *The Law of Peoples with "The Idea of Public Reason Revisited."* (Cambridge, MA: Harvard University Press).

Rawls, John. 2001. *Justice as Fairness: A Restatement*. Ed. Erin Kelly (Cambridge, MA: Belknap Press).

Scanlon, Thomas. 2006. "Justice, Responsibility, and the Demands of Equality." In *The Egalitarian Conscience: Essays in Honour of G.A. Cohen*. Ed. Christine Sypnowich (Oxford: Oxford University Press). Pp. 70–87.

Scheffler, Samuel. 2003. "What Is Egalitarianism?" *Philosophy and Public Affairs* 31: 5–39.

Scheffler, Samuel. 2005. "Choice, Circumstance, and the Value of Equality." *Politics, Philosophy, and Economics* 4: 5–28.

Segall, Shlomi. 2007. "In Solidarity With the Imprudent: A Defense of Luck Egalitarianism." *Social Theory and Practice* 33: 177–98.

Sypnowich, Christine. 2003. "From Marxism to Liberalism (and Back Again)." *Political Studies Review* 1: 333–43.

Sypnowich, Christine. 2014. "A New Approach to Equality." In *Political Neutrality: A Re-evaluation*. Eds. Roberto Merrill and Daniel Weinstock (London: Palgrave-Macmillan). Pp. 178–210.

Tan, Kok-Chor. 2008. "A Defense of Luck Egalitarianism." *The Journal of Philosophy* 105: 665–90.

Tan, Kok-Chor. 2012. *Justice, Institutions, and Luck* (Oxford: Oxford University Press).

Temkin, Larry. 2002. "Equality, Priority, and the Levelling Down Objection." In *The Ideal of Equality*. Eds. Matthew Clayton and Andrew Williams (New York: Palgrave-Macmillan). Pp. 126–61.

Tomlin, Patrick. 2010. "Survey Article: Internal Doubts About Cohen's Rescue of Justice." *The Journal of Political Philosophy* 18: 228–47.

Tomlin, Patrick. 2012. "Can I Be a Luck Egalitarian and a Rawlsian?" *Ethical Perspectives* 19: 371–97.

Valentini, Laura. 2012. "Ideal vs. Non-Ideal Theory: A Conceptual Map." *Philosophy Compass* 7: 654–64.

Watson, Gary. 1989. "Free Agency." In *The Inner Citadel: Essays on Individual Autonomy*. Ed. John Christman (Oxford: Oxford University Press).

Wolff, Jonathan. 1998. "Fairness, Respect, and the Egalitarian Ethos." *Philosophy and Public Affairs* 27: 97–122.

Wolff, Jonathan Wolff. 2010. "Fairness, Respect and the Egalitarian *Ethos* Revisited." *Journal of Ethics* 14: 335–50.

4 Cohen's Equivocal Attack on Rawls's Basic Structure Restriction

1. Introduction

G. A. Cohen is well-known within contemporary political philosophy for his critique of economic incentives,[1] as well as for his related claim that the difference principle extends to the context of personal choice.[2] More recently, he has also received attention for his conceptual claim that justice is a fundamental (and defeasible) value, that is, that justice is one of the normative *inputs* involved in the justificatory process via which action-guiding 'regulatory' principles are selected, rather than the *output*.[3] However, very little effort has been made thus far to explore the possibility of a relationship between these claims.[4] This is surprising. According to Cohen, the difference principle is a derivative, fact-dependent principle, and despite important factual differences between the personal and institutional contexts, he nonetheless maintains that its scope of justified application is wide enough to extend to both. Is there not a tension here, though? It may make sense to think that justice, if a fundamental value, applies to both of these contexts. By contrast, if, like John Rawls, one thinks of it as a set of fact-dependent principles, then the claim that principles of justice suitable for institutions have a wide scope of justified application is prima facie implausible.[5]

In this chapter, I argue that Cohen's attack on the basic structure restriction equivocates across his distinction between fundamental principles of justice, that is, principles that tell us what justice is, and regulatory principles of justice, that is, principles that tell us what is required of us, all things, including justice, considered. Though Cohen initially had the regulatory sense of the word 'justice' in mind when critiquing Rawls's institutional focus, a number of Cohen's replies to Rawls's defenders presuppose Cohen's own, fundamental sense of the word 'justice.' More specifically, in section 3 I argue that Cohen's replies to the problem of demandingness treat the difference principle as if it expresses a defeasible requirement that must be balanced against competing values and as if considerations of measurability are external to its justification. By treating it this way, Cohen seriously compromises the difference principle's clarity; he makes it such that citizens who follow it will often be unable to tell when they have or have not met its requirements. This lack of clarity, in turn, runs afoul of the requirements of publicity and also reduces the difference principle's capacity for 'regulation,' that is, its capacity to guide action.

After making my case for the conclusion that Cohen equivocates, I move on to argue (in section 4) that lack of clarity in a distributive regulatory principle does more than compromise publicity and the capacity for action guidance; it leads to unchosen inequality of burden, too, as some of those who follow it will inadvertently do more than is required of them, and some will inadvertently do less. Collectively, the difficulties associated with lack of clarity suggest we have good reason to prefer an alternative to the difference principle, at least for the context of personal decision making.

In section 5, I discuss the 'profound effect' of a society's institutions on its distribution of benefits and burdens and Cohen's claim that profundity of effect does not exclusively pick out coercive institutions; informal institutions and a society's ethos also have a profound impact on distribution. I also discuss Thomas Pogge's and Joshua Cohen's attempt to defend restricting the direct application of the difference principle to institutions on the grounds that institutions obedient to the difference principle can satisfy its distributive demands, that is, improve the position of the worst-off, in part by affecting the character of its ethos.[6] I argue, not eccentrically I hope, that what is at stake in the choice between direct and indirect application of the difference principle to a society's ethos is whether citizens have a moral obligation to follow said principle in their daily lives. I also claim, on the same grounds as those employed in the previous section, that directly applying a regulatory principle that is clearer than the difference principle but still responsive to efficiency and fundamental justice is a better way to improve the position of the worst-off. I conclude the section by discussing a response from Cohen that, like the personal prerogative and special labor burdens replies, problematically presupposes that the extension of a fundamental value is what's at stake in the issue.

In the final section, I consider Peter Singer's public standard of assistance as a model for such an alternative.[7] Like Cohen's version of the difference principle, Singer's public standard is responsive to the problem posed by demandingness. Unlike Cohen, however, Singer manages to respond to demandingness without also sacrificing clarity. For that reason, Singer's work is worth considering as we try to determine what are the regulatory principles best suited for the personal context.

2. Scope and Status in Cohen's Critique of Rawls

Cohen's canonical objection to the exclusion of personal choice from the scope of distributive justice emerges from his critique of Rawls's use of economic incentives. As most readers of Rawls are aware, the theory of justice he proposes, though largely egalitarian, permits inequalities necessary to facilitate the development and exercise of economically productive talents. Such inequalities are consistent with justice, he claims, when they satisfy the difference principle, that is, when they are necessary to maximally improve the position of the worst-off group in society.[8] Cohen's critique of this position begins with the observation that 'necessary' admits of more than one interpretation. On an intention-independent reading of it, inequalities are only necessary if the talented are literally unable to exercise and develop their talents without them, for example, if those undergoing particularly stressful training required more costly forms of leisure in order to be capable of completing it. Interpreted this way, the word 'necessary' leaves very little room for inequality. On an intention-relative reading, however, it allows for a great deal more, as inequalities created by incentives are now also acceptable.[9] As Cohen indicates, it is the talented themselves who make inequalities of this sort necessary, for it is only necessary to offer incentives if the talented would refrain from raising their economic productivity without them.[10] If this is the case, though, then in what sense can it be said that the talented members of a just society personally affirm its principles? If, as Rawls claims, the citizens of a just society affirm the difference principle and the arguments in favor of it,[11] then how can they consistently make their productivity contingent upon receiving greater benefits? Citizens who believe in the injustice of unnecessary inequalities presumably would not choose to make them necessary by demanding incentives. As such, Cohen maintains that Rawls's endorsement of economic incentives is inconsistent with the ethos his conception of justice incorporates.[12]

In response to the above argument, Cohen contemplates a potential objection that Rawls's supporters might press. According to Rawls, "the primary subject of justice is the basic structure of society", that is, its "political constitution and . . . principal economic and social arrangements."[13] In other words, his principles of justice are specifically intended to apply to institutional structures. If this is so, then there would appear to be nothing inconsistent about affirming the difference principle while also demanding incentive payments. Since its scope is restricted, citizens who affirm it need not apply it to their personal choices.[14]

Cohen's reply to the above line of argument is relatively straightforward. First, he notes that Rawls's stated reason for making the basic structure the subject of justice is the profound impact it has on one's endowment of opportunities and resources, and thus on what one can reasonably expect out of life.[15] Second, he notes that citizens' personal choices collectively also have a profound impact on any individual's endowment of opportunities and resources, in part through their constitutive relationship with informal institutions like the family.[16] His conclusion is that Rawls cannot consistently exclude personal choice from the scope of the difference principle.[17]

It is the above claim in particular—the claim that Rawls cannot consistently endorse the basic structure restriction—that has attracted the most critical attention. Rawls's defenders frequently argue that profundity of effect, though important, is not the only factor relevant to the difference principle's scope of application. They claim that Rawls's endorsement of the basic structure restriction proves to be consistent once other pertinent considerations are taken into account, such as the limits of what justice can reasonably demand from citizens,[18] the requirements of publicity,[19] the causal influence a society's institutions have over its ethos,[20] and so forth.

It will be useful (especially for section 5) to distinguish Cohen's canonical critique of incentives and the basic structure restriction from three other views he holds about the same topics. The first of these views is straightforwardly implied by Cohen's distinction between intention-independent and intention-relative necessity. Since incentives are only required for efficiency insofar as the talented lack the motivation to be just as productive under an equal distribution, the tension between equality and efficiency associated with incentives is a socially contingent one. It is created by the existence of a certain kind of economic ethos and would cease to persist were that ethos to undergo a significant overhaul.

The second view concerns what should be done in cases where a society's social circumstances are such that there is a tension between equality and efficiency. If the prevailing ethos in a society makes the choice between levelling down and equality-upsetting incentives necessary, which of these options should be chosen? For Cohen, the answer is clear. If a choice between permitting incentives and levelling down is inescapable, then permit incentives.[21]

The third view is closely related to Cohen's canonical critique, and is, in fact, expressed in the same piece where he attacks the basic structure restriction on the difference principle. It's the view that a justice-inspired ethos is necessary for a just society.[22] Since the difference between this view and the previously described critique of the basic structure restriction is subtle, it is perhaps worthwhile to devote some effort to articulating it.

In the aforementioned critique of the basic structure restriction, Cohen is specifically challenging the claim that principles suitable for a society's institutional structure should be restricted in scope. Since such restriction would block his claim that citizens' commitment to the difference principle is inconsistent with incentives, Cohen needs to defeat it in order to rescue his critique of incentives from Rawls's defenders. On the basis of Rawls's profundity of effect criterion and the constitutive connection between personal choice and informal institutions, Cohen concludes that institutional principles cannot be restricted in a non-arbitrary fashion. The present view differs from the one expressed in Cohen's canonical critique because it is not committed to symmetry between the institutional and personal contexts. Unlike the canonical view, which advocates extending principles suitable for institutions to the context of personal choice, this view represents the somewhat weaker claim that a just society is necessarily characterized by an ethos of justice in addition to just institutions. Whether the content of the motivations constituting an ethos of justice will be identical to, or somewhat different from, the content of institutional principles, is left open.

So why does Cohen think an ethos of justice is a necessary condition for the justice of a society? Part of his view seems to be that there is something inherent in an ethos of justice that makes it necessary for a just society.[23] The general idea seems to be this: take two societies, both of which have the same institutions and distribution of benefits and burdens, but only one of which is populated by a citizenry who are motivated personally to pursue a just distribution of benefits and burdens. Is the society characterized by the ethos of justice more just than the society that is not so characterized? Cohen thinks the answer is "yes," and thus that the character of a society's ethos counts alongside its institutions and distribution when determining its level of justice. In addition, though, Cohen also seems to think that an ethos of justice is necessary for the justice of a society because of its instrumental relationship with feasibly pursuing a better all-things-considered package of efficiency and equality.[24]

To appreciate this point, it will be helpful to recall the two views I described above, namely, (a) the view that an incentive-related tension between equality and efficiency is socially contingent, and (b) the view that, when required, equality must give way to efficiency in so far as is necessary to avoid levelling down. When considered in tandem, this pair of views suggests that permitting incentives, though the best all-things-considered option under certain circumstances, is nonetheless regrettable, and, at least in the long term, not strictly necessary. An ethos that would allow for a greater amount of equality to be pursued in tandem with efficiency is socially possible and presumably worth pursuing. Given this, when one is asked to compare a society where incentives are necessary to produce the best all-things-considered outcome to a society where, perhaps because of social change, they are not, shouldn't one be able to say that the latter is more just than the former? Both societies are all-things-considered optimal, but one society's ethos allows for the realization of greater equality in its all-things-considered package. Were the character of a society's institutions the only thing making up its justice, however, we would be unable to recognize the differing degrees of justice exemplified by these two possibilities; that is, the degree of justice exemplified by these societies would necessarily be identical.

As I mentioned in the introduction, my argument in the next section is that Cohen's attack on the basic structure restriction equivocates across his distinction between fundamental justice and regulatory justice; though his canonical critique is about the scope of regulatory 'justice,' a number of his replies to Rawls's defenders presuppose the fundamental sense of the word 'justice.' To better understand why, though, it will be helpful to first say a bit about the conceptual critique of Rawls that Cohen launched in the later part of his career.

According to Cohen's conceptual critique, Rawls is wrong to think that specifying the content of justice is a matter of specifying principles suitable for guiding political practice. On Cohen's view, justice is a fundamental value, that is, one of the normative *inputs* involved in the justificatory process via which action guiding institutional principles are selected, rather than the *output*.[25] This claim is embedded in a pluralistic picture of the meta-ethical universe. For Cohen, morality is comprised of a plurality of irreducible, fundamental values that sometimes conflict with each other.[26] As a result, any principle expressing the content of a fundamental value, such as a principle of efficiency, a principle of community, a principle of compassion, and so on, is only indirectly normative on Cohen's view. Such a principle tells us how to evaluate a society with respect to one of the moral elements in light of which it is or is not morally desirable, but it cannot by itself tell a legislator what to *do*.[27] To identify justice as a fundamental value, then, is to identify it as a tool directly useful for evaluating the justice or injustice of a society, but only indirectly useful for determining how a society ought to be run. Prescribing institutional arrangements requires formulating what Cohen calls 'rules of regulation,' that is, formulating derivative principles, the content of which reflect considerations other than just justice, such as considerations of efficiency, stability, compassion, and so forth.[28]

Two characteristics of fundamental justice implicit in the above description are worth highlighting before we move on to the next section. It is in light of these characteristics that Cohen's replies to critics are sometimes equivocal. The first is that fundamental justice is defeasible. As one value within a pluralistic moral universe, fundamental justice is subject to trade-offs. Unlike regulatory justice, which represents the weightings we have assigned to competing values, fundamental justice is one of the values that must be weighed, and we must be careful not to accord it an excessive degree of moral significance.

The second characteristic of interest is that many considerations are external to fundamental justice. In Cohen's view, much that is morally significant is nonetheless irrelevant to justifying a conception of fundamental justice.[29] Cohen's view on this matter is partially traceable to his value pluralism. Fairness, community, efficiency, compassion, and so on are all different values, and it is important that considerations belonging to one be kept separate from the others when filling out their content. In addition, though, it is traceable to his exclusiveness about justice, that is, to his view that justice is a relatively simple value rather than a complex value with many internal aspects. Undoubtedly fairness is an internal consideration; if something is unfair, then it is also, to that extent, unjust.[30] Furthermore, in Cohen's view, egalitarianism supplies the right conception of fairness in distribution, specifically luck egalitarianism.[31] Though Cohen sometimes seems to think that nothing but fairness is internal to justice, and thus that any conflict between fairness and other moral considerations is a conflict between justice and non-justice considerations, there are places where he relaxes this narrowness somewhat. In *Why not Socialism?* he expresses some uncertainty about whether community is internal to justice,[32] and in "Fairness and Legitimacy in Justice" he concedes that justice also has a historical component that he, as the title suggests, calls 'legitimacy.'[33] Notwithstanding these exceptions, Cohen's view of what qualifies as a consideration of justice is a narrow one that excludes many considerations, such as efficiency, measurability, stability, and so on. Such considerations are pertinent to justifying principles of regulation, in his view, but they are external to the project of justifying a conception of fundamental justice.

In the next section, I will chart some of the literary terrain surrounding Cohen's critique of incentives and Rawls's basic structure restriction. In particular, I will focus on the literature surrounding the worry that applying the difference principle in the context of personal choice is excessively demanding. Cohen's replies to this worry presuppose that when he uses the term 'justice,' he has in mind a particular fundamental value. Unfortunately, the issue he and his opponents are debating is not whether a fundamental value extends to the context of personal choice, but whether the difference principle does, and, as we have noted, the difference principle is a regulatory *output* intended to guide institutional design, not a justificatory *input*.

3. Demandingness, Subjective Welfare, and Cohen's Personal Prerogative

An important difference between the contexts of institutional design and personal choice is that people, unlike institutions, have personal lives. In light of this, the requirement that citizens embody the difference principle in their everyday lives appears rather demanding. It seems to entail that well-off citizens are morally required to devote a tremendous amount of their time and energy to helping the worst-off.[34] To fully appreciate this worry, it is helpful to consider the kinds of behaviour Cohen's ethos would motivate. On the one hand, an ethos can contribute to the justness of a distribution by supplementing institutional measures. Supplementation, according to Cohen, occurs when ethos-motivated actions, such as making personal donations or volunteering during one's spare time, are pursued independently of public justice–seeking measures. Enhancement, in contrast, is ethos-motivated action that's conjoined with public justice–seeking measures. Such would include, for instance, continuing to work just as hard under a radical tax regime as one would under a less radical one, or choosing to take on an economically productive profession for which one's talents are well-suited in spite of the fact that said tax regime disallows incentives.[35] Examples like these highlight just how pervasive Cohen's ethos would be if realized. It would ostensibly require one to prioritize the worst-off whenever distributive considerations are relevant, and there are a great many situations where they are.

Cohen's reply to the above worry is not dismissive. He attempts to accommodate it by qualifying his ethos with a personal prerogative to pursue other matters, such as self-interest, expressing affection to one's loved ones, non-justice moral commitments, and so on.[36] As such, an individual who finds himself in possession of extra cash might legitimately choose to keep a portion of it for some purpose other than benefitting the worst-off, and someone who would make an exceptional engineer might justifiably choose a different career, so long as these choices do not exceed the bounds of a reasonable (and unspecified) limit on the extent to which deviating from the difference principle is permissible.[37] But even if his ethos were not so qualified, Cohen claims that it would only require a work-till-you-drop duty if one mistakenly leaves subjective welfare out of one's metric. If one's metric incorporates subjective welfare in addition to resources, then inequalities in resource endowment will sometimes be justified in order to compensate the talented for their labor burdens.[38]

Furthermore, including welfare means those with greater talents need not enslave themselves to the betterment of the worse-off if doing so would require sacrificing too much of it. The talented, should they become sufficiently miserable, would themselves become the worst-off group, so it cannot be said that a welfare-inclusive metric would require them to utterly devote themselves to promoting the betterment of the untalented.[39]

In his article "Incentives, Inequality, and Publicity," Andrew Williams argues that Cohen's difference principle–based ethos is incapable of meeting Rawls's publicity condition, that is, that citizens who embrace it will not be able to discern when and where the requirements of the ethos have been adequately satisfied. Williams offers a number of considerations in support of this conclusion, but many revolve around the inclusion of subjective welfare and Cohen's personal prerogative qualification. As Williams correctly notes, determining whether an individual with greater-than-average resources has satisfied her justice-related duties requires checking to see whether her extra wealth either compensates for labor burdens or is consistent with a legitimate personal prerogative.[40] In order to check the first of these, one must be able to interpersonally compare levels of job satisfaction. Unfortunately, doing so appears to be beyond our epistemic abilities. Distinguishing the effect of someone's occupation on her welfare from the effects of other welfare-impacting factors in her personal life is very difficult. What's more, self-deception about job satisfaction is common.[41] As a result, acquiring the information needed to reliably determine which of those with more resources are 'burdened' by their jobs is extremely difficult, especially on a society-wide scale.

Equally difficult is determining whether the greater-resourced have exceeded the bounds of a legitimate personal prerogative. At what point does deviating from the pursuit of justice for the sake of other projects cease to be permissible? Cohen does not attempt to specify this, and the reason for that may be because the answer might vary from person to person depending on their personal history, circumstances, and so on.[42]

In sum, Cohen's replies to the problem of demandingness make an ethos based on the difference principle more palatable, but at the cost of citizens being unable to determine whether their co-citizens are fulfilling their duties. In fact, the above-mentioned difficulties suggest that a citizen will have difficulty telling whether she has fulfilled her duties (Am *I* 'burdened' by my job relative to others? When does the pursuit of *my* self-interest become impermissible?).

As worrisome as Williams's objections are, they become even more worrisome when we are reminded that the difference principle, in Cohen's view, is a regulatory principle that reflects, but is distinct from, justice itself. Its function is not to tell us what justice is, but to tell us what we ought to do, all things, including justice, considered. If this is the function of a distributive regulatory principle, though, then being unable to tell whether one has successfully followed it clearly undermines that function. This is especially obvious with respect to the idea of a personal prerogative in particular. To see what I have in mind, consider again Cohen's discussion of how competing values operate. Rawls's mistake, Cohen claims, is allowing non-justice considerations to influence the content of his conception of justice. Since justice is a fundamental value, other values such as efficiency or compassion specifically limit the weight it can reasonably be accorded when adopting distributive regulatory principles; that is, they constrain justice's *implementation*, not its *content*. If this is the manner in which external values relate to justice, however, then there is a tension between Cohen's conceptual critique of the difference principle and his claim that the demands it imposes are constrained by a personal prerogative. Since the difference principle is regulatory and thus allegedly distinct from justice itself, its content should be justified in light of the various considerations that must be given weight in the personal context. If, upon reflection, we decide that strictly adhering to the difference principle would not leave enough space for self-interest, affection, and the various moral considerations that stand prominent in the personal context (loyalty to friends, for example), then we have reason to adopt another principle better tailored for the personal realm instead. Cohen's strategy of retaining the difference principle but constraining it with a personal prerogative is responsive to the importance of leaving space for self-interest, personal moral commitments, and so on, but his strategy also deprives the difference principle of its capacity for action guidance by requiring us to balance it against competing considerations in much the same manner that we balance conflicting values against each other. As a result, Cohen's personal prerogative qualification treats the difference principle as if it is a principle of fundamental justice, and thus it constitutes an equivocal reply to the demandingness objection.

A further instance of equivocation is identifiable in Cohen's rationale for including subjective welfare in the difference principle's metric. In a footnote from Chapter 2 of *Rescuing Justice and Equality*, Cohen writes: "Had I written the article that is the substance of the present chapter after I had reached the distinction drawn in Chapter 6 between fundamental principles and rules of regulation, I would have said that labor burdens must come into the assessment of fundamental justice, however difficult it may be to represent them, even by proxy, within rules of regulation."[43] Why does Cohen think that fundamental justice requires accounting for labor burdens? To understand the answer, it will be helpful to recall our discussion of internality and externality in the previous section and in section 3 of Chapter 2. As previously noted, Cohen and I think it is important that considerations belonging to one fundamental value be kept separate from considerations belonging to others when formulating conceptions of their content. With respect to justice in particular, judgments of fairness are internal, while most other judgments, such as judgments of efficiency, are external. As a result, if judgments of fairness direct us to include subjective welfare in the metric of our conception of fundamental justice, thus making it responsive to labor burdens, then we presumably ought to do so. Cohen's favored judgment to this effect is the one associated with the wheelchair-bound individual in "On the Currency of Egalitarian Justice." This person is able to raise his arms, but he is unable to do so without experiencing considerable discomfort. Since it makes no sense to represent this inability as a deficiency in physical resources, Cohen deems (correctly, I think) that the egalitarian intuition to compensate him, ceteris paribus, for the sake of fairness, springs from his relative lack of subjective welfare.[44] Unfortunately for Cohen, though, this observation amounts to another instance of equivocation in the present case. Though we have good reason to think that subjective welfare is part of the metric of fundamental justice, the difference principle is not a conception of fundamental justice. It is a regulatory principle, and regulatory principles, in order to be effective guides to action, must be concerned with accurate interpersonal comparisons. Unlike with fundamental justice, measurability is not external to regulatory justice, and thus we have good reason to exclude subjective welfare from our regulatory metric.

The above points hopefully suffice to demonstrate that Cohen's subjective welfare and personal prerogative replies to the demandingness objection equivocate across his distinction between fundamental and regulatory justice. Though Cohen's initial discussion of the scope of justice concerned the extension of institutional regulatory principles to personal choice, a number of his replies to critics suggest that by the term 'justice' he has in mind a fundamental value, that is, a relatively simple, defeasible concept that must be balanced against competing considerations before arriving at an all-things-considered conclusion about what to do. As I have already noted, including welfare and adding a personal prerogative deprive the difference principle of its capacity for action guidance. Difficulties with interpersonally comparing levels of job satisfaction make it impossible to accurately judge when compensation for labor burdens is warranted and determining the extent to which a personal prerogative justifies deviating from the difference principle is nearly as difficult. In short, the requirements of a welfare-inclusive, prerogative-constrained difference principle are not sufficiently clear for those who follow it to be able to tell when they have done enough for the worst-off.

It should be noted that Cohen's reflections on the relationship between publicity and fundamental justice confirm that he ought to be sympathetic to my worries about clarity. On the one hand, he denies that publicity is a constraint on the content of fundamental justice. He correctly notes that an action or policy may qualify as just even if it is not possible to tell that it is, in fact, just. He does maintain, however, that publicity is a desideratum relevant to the implementation of justice, or, in other words, that it is a consideration that good regulatory principles must be responsive to. He even notes that it is sometimes appropriate to prioritize publicity over fundamental justice in cases where the two come into conflict. As such, the lack of clarity associated with a welfare-inclusive, prerogative-constrained difference principle is problematic in light of a desideratum that Cohen himself affirms.[45]

To be fair, the fact that a regulatory principle lacks clarity is not necessarily a decisive strike against it. Clarity, because of its relationship with publicity and action guidance, is an important desideratum of regulatory principles, but that is different from being a strict constraint. As with other desiderata, it is reasonable to trade off clarity against competing considerations, and thus it might be argued that Cohen's version of the difference principle is justified in spite of the difficulties I have raised.[46] However, it must be acknowledged that lack of clarity is a drawback. Ceteris paribus, a clear regulatory principle is better than an unclear one.[47] Furthermore, I think that lack of clarity is a more significant problem than it may appear to be at first glance. Combined with the concerns I have raised in this section, the connection I draw in the next section between clarity and distributive fairness should suffice to undermine Cohen's claim that the difference principle is suitable for the context of personal choice.

4. Clarity and Fairness

Thus far, we've discussed two reasons for why the clarity of a regulatory principle matters. One reason is that the function of a regulatory principle is to guide action, and a lack of clarity undermines this. Another reason is that a lack of clarity compromises publicity. A further reason not yet discussed is that attempting to follow an unclear principle has distributive consequences. Some people will inadvertently do more than is required of them, and some will inadvertently do less; this in turn leads to unfairness. A good way to understand the unfairness I have in mind is with reference to Cohen's (and my) favorite conception of distributive fairness: luck egalitarianism. When the luck egalitarian standard is used to evaluate the effects of applying the difference principle to personal choice, it is clear that there is an important sense in which the difference principle falls short of it. Since committed citizens are unable to determine when they have done enough to fulfill the requirements of a welfare-inclusive, prerogative-constrained difference principle, the regulatory application of said principle to personal choice runs contrary to luck equality in an important way. Its lack of clarity inevitably yields unchosen inequality in the distribution of burden, as some people will inadvertently take on a greater burden than is required of them by the difference principle, while others will inadvertently take on a lesser burden than is required of them. Of course, the difference principle, as a regulatory principle, always falls short of perfect fairness. This is because taking all things into consideration means deviating from the requirements of fairness for the sake feasibility and competing values. The unfairness I have identified is different, however. It does not lie in the fact that the difference principle is insensitive to differences between members of the worst-off group or in the fact that it allows for necessary inequalities between differently talented citizens, but rather in the effect its unclear application to personal choice has on the distribution of burden. An ethos based on the difference principle thus deviates from luck equality in a way that is independent from the familiar, content-specific deviations.

It might be objected that ethotic commitment to the Difference Principle is always a matter of choice, just as any unenforced moral requirement is. If so, then how are inequalities in the level of ethotic contribution to the worst-off unfair? Citizens choose whether to commit themselves to the difference principle, and thus any accidental inequality in the associated distribution of burden is produced by option luck.[48]

Though it is true that citizens choose whether or not to apply the difference principle in their personal lives, I do not think it is appropriate to treat inequalities indirectly associated with the choice to commit one's self to the difference principle as standard cases of option luck inequality. In standard cases of option luck, the choices made are not supposed to be morally obligatory. Whether the poker player decides to bet her money or merely play for fun is her prerogative. The naturally talented follower of the difference principle, in contrast, has an alleged moral duty to promote the interests of the worst-off. What's more, unlike the voluntarily acquired duties associated with contracts or friendships, her duty is a product of her circumstances. After all, the talented person did not choose to have the natural capacities she does, and thus did not choose to be put in a position where doing the right thing would require that she make voluntary sacrifices. As a result, she cannot be held responsible in the usual way for the consequences of her choice to follow the difference principle.

The problem I have raised here is similar to a problem raised by Susan Hurley. Like me, Hurley argues that there is a tension between Cohen's luck egalitarianism and his canonical critique of Rawls. More specifically, she claims that there is a tension between (a) claiming that inequalities traceable to choice should remain intact and (b) claiming that justice prohibits providing incentives and yet requires the talented to work just as hard as they counter-factually would have.[49] On the plausible assumption that the productivity of the talented is at least partially traceable to their choices (an assumption that is actually presupposed by the claim that the talented are morally required to work just as hard without incentives), does not luck egalitarianism suggest that the talented are entitled to a larger portion of the extra goods generated by their efforts? It seems that luck egalitarians are committed to saying as much, since it is unfair, on their view, to eliminate inequalities traceable to choice.

Cohen's reply to Hurley is fairly simple. He maintains that a choice-based justification for socio-economic inequality is different from an incentive-based justification, and that his critique of incentives only condemns the latter.[50] In other words, while a personal commitment to the difference principle would not permit talented workers to *make* incentives necessary by refusing to work just as hard without them, nothing prevents those workers from concluding that they are entitled to more resources than those who work less. Of course, such a justification would also apply to hardworking citizens who lack productive talents, and thus it is a justification for socio-economic inequality between those who choose to work hard and those who choose not to, rather than a justification for inequality between the talented and the untalented.

Though Cohen is right to distinguish choice-based justifications for (non-luck) inequality from incentive-based justifications, it seems to me that citizens committed to the difference principle are required to reject the former just as much as they are required to reject the latter. After all, the difference principle does not distinguish between those who are worse off due to choice and those who are worse off due to bad luck. Though fair equality of opportunity and a concern for mitigating the distributive effects of the genetic lottery are broadly consistent with the requirements of luck equality, the difference principle is not a form of luck egalitarianism. Unlike a principle of luck equality, it is insensitive to choice-related differences between members of the same socio-economic class; it simply specifies that any inequalities must be necessary to benefit those who have less, regardless of why they have less. As a result, the difference principle condemns unnecessary inequality of any sort, not just between the talented and the untalented, but also between those who work hard and those who do not. The upshot is that citizens who accept rewards on the grounds that they have chosen to work harder than others would be permitting an unnecessary inequality. In light of this, it seems to me that we have yet another way in which an ethos based on the difference principle deviates from the requirements of luck equality. Not only would such an ethos create unchosen inequality in the distribution of burden between those committed to it, but it denies them a choice-based justification for retaining extra resources. Of course, Cohen's version of the difference principle is a bit different from the standard version. As we have noted throughout, his difference principle is a welfare-inclusive, prerogative-constrained principle. As such, it is consistent with both personal prerogative- and labor burdens–based justifications for retaining extra resources, even if it is not consistent with incentive- or choice-based justifications. Whether or not the amount justified by a personal prerogative or by compensation for labor burdens would be less than the amount justified by a choice-based justification is difficult to say. However, the fact that the hardworking talented are able to retain extra resources via alternative justificatory routes suggests that unchosen inequality of burden is the more pressing deviation from luck equality.

Unfairness is always regrettable, but it may also be the case that a certain amount of unfairness in the distribution of regulatory burden is unavoidable in the personal context. If so, then so be it. Shouldn't we try to minimize this unfairness insofar as we can, though? Is it possible to leave space for affection, self-interest, loyalty, and so on without also sacrificing clarity? In section 6, I examine Peter Singer's public standard of assistance in hopes of shedding some light on what a clear, easy-to-follow alternative might look like. My goal is not so much to defend Singer's standard, but rather to draw attention to its virtues so that they might be taken into consideration in future efforts to determine what, exactly, are the regulatory principles best suited for the personal context. Before turning to Singer, however, I first discuss another issue pertaining to Cohen's critique of Rawls's basic structure restriction: the causal relationship between institutions and a society's ethos.

5. Causing Justice

In section 3, I hope to have successfully argued that Cohen's replies to the demandingness objection assume, for the most part, that the position under attack by his critics is the extension of fundamental justice, rather than the extension of regulatory justice. Though the inclusion of welfare in the metric of egalitarian justice is supported by considerations of fairness and would suffice to alleviate justice's demands on the choices of the talented, considerations of fairness do not have the same decisiveness for conceptions of regulatory justice that they do for conceptions of fundamental justice. Regulatory principles are sensitive to facts about measurability, and thus the difficulties associated with interpersonal comparisons of subjective welfare are a good reason not to directly include it.

Furthermore, though the implementation of fundamental justice is subject to trade-offs with the normative considerations represented by a personal prerogative, regulatory principles do not work this way. They are adopted in light of the various normative considerations that must be given weight in a particular context, and thus those considerations should not be represented as constraints upon or desiderata in competition with what is adopted. Including welfare in the metric of regulatory principles, and intuitively balancing them against competing considerations, compromises regulatory principles' capacity for action guidance by making their demands less clear than they otherwise would be. A clearer alternative to the difference principle is preferable for the context of personal choice.

Another issue that has received a notable amount of attention in the literature surrounding Cohen's canonical critique of Rawls is the causal relationship between a society's institutions, ethos, and distribution. Recall that Rawls's profundity of effect criterion plays a pivotal role in Cohen's argument. Cohen notes that Rawls's focus on a society's basic structure is justified by institutions' profound effect on the distribution of benefits and burdens. Cohen then goes on to argue that the criterion also applies to citizens' personal choices and is thus too expansive to support the basic structure restriction. This criticism is interesting in part because it draws on a criterion that Rawls himself endorses. For our purposes, it is also interesting because of its explicit regulatory character. As we have already noted, regulatory principles connect fundamental values to political practice by telling us what is to be done once trade-offs and feasibility have been accounted for. Given that this is the function of regulatory principles, it is natural that we should take into consideration their expected effects. In Cohen's words, "we adopt them [regulatory principles] in light of what we expect the effect of adopting them to be."[51]

Since designing our institutions in accordance with the difference principle would presumably generate a stable distribution that is largely egalitarian and reasonably efficient to boot, there is good reason to adopt the difference principle in the institutional context. If applying the difference principle to personal choice would likely have the effect of generating a distribution with these virtues plus an even greater degree of equality, then there is good reason to adopt it for the context of personal choice too. Employing Rawls's profundity of effect criterion in the manner Cohen does thus straightforwardly supports the claim that the scope of regulatory justice should be extended.

In well-known articles, Thomas Pogge and Joshua Cohen challenge the claim that the profundity of effect criterion is inconsistent with the basic structure restriction.[52] The main idea behind both of their arguments is that the basic structure's effect on distribution is partially mediated by the effects of a host of other factors. Institutions that successfully conform to the difference principle do so by producing a distribution in which the least well-off are as well-off as they can be, but the manner in which it does so inevitably involves a variety of causal mechanisms, such as technology, demographics, *social ethos*, and so on.[53] The relationship between institutions and the development of a society's ethos is especially important here. G. A. Cohen has certainly demonstrated that the character of a society's ethos has important distributive effects, but as J. Cohen explains at some length, the character of a society's institutions has a powerful effect on the character of its ethos.

By way of example, J. Cohen explains that there is evidence suggesting that the choice between 'consensual' democratic institutions and 'majoritarian' democratic institutions has ethos-related implications. Adopting new policies in a 'consensual' framework requires a greater degree of support across political parties and interest groups than it does in the latter framework and, as a result, consensual frameworks tend to foster an ethos of solidarity and inclusivity.[54] If Pogge's and J. Cohen's general point holds true, then Rawls can acknowledge the profound impact of ethos on distribution without giving up either the basic structure restriction or the profundity of effect criterion. He can maintain that direct application of the difference principle is restricted to the basic structure, yet acknowledge that his conception of justice requires adopting institutional alternatives even when they improve the position of the worst-off via their influence on the prevailing ethos. The distributive significance of a society's ethos is thus accounted for without directly applying the difference principle to personal choice.

The first move G. A. Cohen makes in reply to this criticism is to accept that institutions causally influence a society's ethos while denying that they are causally independent of it. Just as institutions affect ethos, so too does ethos affect institutions, so why restrict the difference principle to institutions on causal grounds?[55] If the position of the worst-off can be improved by modifying a society's ethos in ways that will positively affect its institutions, then presumably the difference principle requires those modifications. To deny this, yet maintain that the difference principle requires modifying institutions when doing so will affect a society's ethos in ways that benefit the worst-off, involves inconsistently applying the profundity of effect criterion.

G. A. Cohen's first reply to J. Cohen and Pogge has the virtue of being free of equivocation, but I do not think either he or his critics really to get to the heart of what is at stake in the issue. First, I presume that any Rawlsian who takes Rawls's 'natural duty of justice' even half-seriously would agree that a society's ethos is capable of affecting its institutions. Were it not, then a civic duty to "further just [institutional] arrangements not yet established" would be infeasible.[56] The question at hand is not so much whether a society's institutional arrangements are causally independent of its ethos (which they almost certainly are not), but whether the difference principle should directly regulate citizens' personal choices. What does it mean for the difference principle to directly regulate personal choice? As far as I can tell, the difference between direct and indirect regulation lies in what citizens are obligated to do. If the difference principle applies directly to personal choice, then citizens who fail to follow it in their personal lives have failed to fulfill an all-things-considered moral requirement. As such, direct application of the difference principle to personal choice entails that it is appropriate to condemn the behavior of those who do not comply with it.

In contrast, indirectly applying the difference principle to personal choice via the ethos-affecting impact of institutional change lacks this implication. Behavior that has the effect of promoting the same state of affairs at which the difference principle aims would presumably be widespread in a society whose institutions were chosen on the basis of their causal relationship with a worst off–improving ethos, but one could not say that individuals who choose not to apply the difference principle, or who apply it on some occasions but not others, have thereby done something wrong. At best, one could say that those citizens who do choose to adhere to the difference principle are praiseworthy, and that it is regrettable some citizens have chosen not to. Of course, if there is an alternative institutional arrangement that would successfully promote an even greater degree of worst off–improving behavior, then the difference principle would require implementing it. Still, to say that a society's institutions have failed to meet the requirements of regulatory justice is not the same as saying that its citizens have, except insofar as its citizens have failed in their responsibility to implement better institutions.

With this understanding of the distinction between direct and indirect application in mind, the best reasons available for rejecting that the difference principle justifiably applies in a direct fashion to personal choice are, in my opinion, those I have already gone over in the previous section. As I hope to have established, an ethos that is both based on the direct application of the difference principle and capable of escaping the demandingness objection is also unclear in its demands, and thus it has a reduced capacity for action guidance. What's more, a practical upshot of this lack of clarity is unfairness in the contribution levels of those committed to it (some will inadvertently do more than their fair share, and some will inadvertently do less). All things considered, whichever regulatory principle(s) we do adopt for the direct regulation of personal choice should be clearer than a welfare-inclusive, prerogative-constrained difference principle. In contrast, indirect commitment to the difference principle avoids this issue. Since in that case the talented are not morally obligated to follow it, they cannot say that their circumstances put them in a position where rightness required voluntary self-sacrifice of them. Any inequality in contribution produced by the difference principle's lack of clarity would be no more unfair than inequality in contribution to a charitable cause.

An interesting issue for the above-mentioned account is raised by the possibility that an alternative institutional arrangement could further improve the position of the worst-off via deception. After all, if everyone thought that they had to follow the difference principle as a matter of moral obligation, then presumably the position of the worst-off would be more improved than if everyone knew that such behavior is praiseworthy but not all-things-considered required. Thankfully, Rawls's publicity condition can be used to rule out this unsavory possibility. Any attempt to raise the position of the worst-off via deception can presumably be ruled out on the same publicity-related grounds as government-house utilitarianism. At the same time, though, an institutional framework that encourages commitment to the difference principle in one's personal life on the grounds that commitment to it is merely praiseworthy seems unlikely to be very effective.

The combination of these points suggests to me that the most-effective, publicity-consistent way for institutions to improve the position of the worst-off via impact on ethos is by encouraging commitment to the regulatory principles citizens actually are morally obligated to adhere to, the effects of which will overlap to some extent with what commitment to the difference principle would achieve (these principles must still give weight to equality and efficiency, after all). As I will suggest in the next section, it may be the case that better-off citizens should, among other things, adopt a norm that requires them to donate a determinate percentage of their income, with the richest of the better-off being required to donate the highest percentage and the less wealthy among them being required to donate a lower percentage.[57] Widespread commitment to such a requirement would presumably succeed at improving the position of the worst-off, would provide much clearer guidance than a directly applied difference principle, and would likely be more effective at helping the worst-off than a non-obligatory difference principle. Interestingly, promoting an obligatory alternative to the difference principle that has overlapping effects simultaneously counts as indirect application of the difference principle and direct application of an alternative to it, thus unifying the regulatory principles for institutions with the regulatory principles for individuals in a way that permits different content for each.

Thus far I have argued that G. A. Cohen's reply to Pogge and J. Cohen, that is, his claim that a society's ethos affects its institutions too, misses what is at stake in the issue between them. On all counts, citizens have a civic responsibility to ensure that their institutions conform to the difference principle, and thus whether an ethos can causally affect institutions is not at issue. What is at issue is whether citizens have a moral obligation to pursue the difference principle, rather than some other distributive regulatory principle, in their daily lives. I have argued that we have reason to doubt this. However, G. A. Cohen has a second reply to Pogge and J. Cohen, a reply that I will now proceed to address.

According to G. A. Cohen's second reply, questions about the causal relationship between a society's institutions and its social ethos are not at the heart of the issue. The real question at hand in the debate over whether justice extends to personal choice is not what *causes* a society to be just, but rather what *constitutes* its justice. He claims that even if it is true that the basic structure is the primary causal factor determining both the character of a society's ethos and the distribution of benefits and burdens, this does not mean that the justice of a society is constituted *solely* by the justice of its institutions. What is at stake in the constitution question is whether the justice of other features of a society must be taken into account when assessing whether the society is just as a whole.[58]

To better perceive the distinction between causing and constituting justice, recall our discussion (in section 2) of Cohen's two reasons for thinking that an ethos of justice is necessary for a just society. The first of these reasons was that there is something intrinsic to an ethos that makes it necessary. If we take two hypothetical societies, both of which have the same institutions and distribution of benefits and burdens, but only one of which is populated by a citizenry who are motivated to pursue a just distribution of benefits and burden via the choices they make in their personal lives, it seems that we should evaluate the society characterized by an ethos of justice as more just that the society that is not so characterized. This consideration supports the claim that the justice of a society's ethos is part of what *constitutes* the justice of the society. By contrast, part of what makes an ethos of justice necessary for the justice of a society is its instrumental relationship with a better all-things-considered package of efficiency and equality. If we compare a society where incentives are necessary to produce the best all-things-considered outcome to a society whose ethos makes incentives unnecessary, it seems that we should evaluate the latter society as more just than the former. Both societies are all-things-considered optimal, but one society's social circumstances allow for the realization of greater equality in its all-things-considered package. This consideration supports the claim that an ethos of justice, because of its impact on a factor that partially constitutes the justice of a society (its distribution), is an integral part of what *causes* the justice of a society.

To illustrate how this point applies to Pogge's and J. Cohen's defense of the basic structure restriction, G. A. Cohen asks us to imagine a society whose institutions are governed by the difference principle in the manner Pogge and J. Cohen have in mind. This society's institutions seek to eliminate any inequality in benefits and burdens not needed to improve the position of the worst-off, and it sometimes does so through its influence over the society's ethos. Suppose that certain inequalities in this society are ineliminable because certain features of its ethos cannot feasibly be changed. On the J. Cohen and Pogge view, this society is perfectly just, as there is no feasible institutional change that could cause more equality without worsening the position of the worst-off. That their view requires deeming this society to be perfectly just is, according to G. A. Cohen, a serious drawback, though, for recognizing the fact that a degree of unfairness persists in this society, and thus that it is sub-optimally just, is important. Insofar as the society is sub-optimally just because the ineliminable problems with its ethos are intrinsically regrettable, the Pogge/J. Cohen position is problematic because it fails to recognize that a society's ethos is part of what constitutes its justice. Insofar as the society is sub-optimally just because the ineliminable problems with its ethos are extrinsically regrettable (regrettable because we cannot improve the prevailing distribution without changing the society's ethos), the Pogge/J. Cohen position is problematic because it fails to recognize that a society's distribution affects its justice independently of what its institutions can or cannot feasibly cause.[59] Either way, the problem is supposed to demonstrate that a society's justice is constituted by more than the justice of its institutions.

G. A. Cohen's distinction between what causes and what constitutes the justice of a society is sound, and his reply to Pogge's and J. Cohen's defense of the basic structure restriction is sharp. Unfortunately, it represents another instance of equivocation on his part. Recall once more that the difference principle is a regulatory principle and that regulatory principles are sensitive to feasibility constraints. Though G. A. Cohen's right to emphasize the importance of recognizing that ineliminable inequality renders a society imperfectly just, this only holds true in the fundamental sense of 'justice.' The content of fundamental justice is insensitive to facts about what is or is not feasible, so fundamental justice recognizes the unfairness of even those inequalities which cannot feasibly be removed. Regulatory justice, in contrast, is about what, all things considered, ought to be done or implemented, and one of the things that must be considered when adopting all-things-considered principles is feasibility. A society with an ineliminable inequality traceable to unmodifiable features of its ethos, such as widespread psychological incapacities that are impossible to overcome, is still all-things-considered optimal as long as that ethos is as just as it can feasibly be, and so long as all eliminable inequalities have been removed. Ineliminable intrinsic unfairness in a society's ethos should be recognized via the evaluative application of fundamental justice, but such unfairness cannot be said to constitute an all-things-considered regulatory shortcoming. Similarly, ineliminable extrinsic unfairness in a society's ethos, that is, ineliminable unfairness in the distribution of benefits and burden traceable to its ethos, should also be recognized via the evaluative application of fundamental justice, but such unfairness cannot be said to constitute an all-things-considered regulatory shortcoming. Put another way, you cannot reasonably condemn people for failing to pursue justice past the point where it is psychologically impossible for them to do more.

To further drive the point home, let us return to the intuitive thought experiments meant to support the claim that an ethos of justice is necessary for the justice of a society, but let us be explicit this time about when we have regulatory justice in mind and when we have fundamental justice in mind. First, we noted that if we take two hypothetical societies, both of which have the same institutions and distribution of benefits and burdens, but only one of which has an ethos of justice, that we should evaluate the society with an ethos of justice as more just than the society without this ethos. Is this true when we have specifically the regulatory sense of justice in mind? It seems not. From a regulatory perspective, the difference between these two societies is that the citizens of one do not aim to promote distributive justice via their personal choices, while the citizens of the others do but are entirely ineffective. Given that regulatory rules are assessed in light of their effects, it would be strange to say that the society that impotently extends its regulatory rules to the personal context has achieved anything greater than the society that does not bother to do so. In other words, the fact that the pursuit of regulatory principles in citizens' personal lives is ineffective in this case undermines the justified application of the relevant principles to the personal context; that is, citizens in the ethos-possessing society are not obligated to follow the rules they do. However, there is something admirable about the intentions of those who try to promote distributive justice despite the futility of the rules they follow. They value and are motivated by a concern for fairness, that is, by a concern for the promotion of fundamental justice, and it seems natural enough to acknowledge the desirability of this when evaluating their motives. From the perspective of fundamental justice, then, there seems to be a difference between how these societies should be evaluated, even if the effects of their regulatory measures are identical.

With respect to the second intuitive thought experiment—the one where we compare a society in which incentives are necessary to produce the best all-things-considered outcome to a society whose ethos makes incentives unnecessary—the comparative judgments we render will depend on how different these societies are. On the one hand, suppose that the citizens in the society with more inequality cannot, for some reason or another, feasibly do more in their personal lives than they currently are doing (perhaps they all share some psychologically limiting gene that citizens in the more-equal society lack). In that case, there is literally no all-things-considered difference between these societies. No feasible institutional alternative could be implemented in the less-equal society to change its ethos, and its citizens cannot be obligated do that which is psychologically impossible for them, so the less-equal society is all-things-considered optimal, just as the more-equal society is. The only morally relevant difference between them is that one, regrettably but only regrettably, has an inegalitarian ethos and thus a less-equal distribution. The less-equal society exhibits less commitment to fairness in its ethos and less realized fairness in its distribution, and is thus less just when measured against the bar of specifically fundamental justice.

On the other hand, suppose the society with less equality can feasibly improve its ethos but just has not taken the measures necessary to do so. In that case, insofar as those measures could be implemented institutionally, the society's institutions fall short of what the difference principle requires. Furthermore, since citizens are psychologically capable of doing more, we can also condemn them insofar as they have a reasonable moral obligation that they are failing to fulfill. This moral obligation may not be constituted by an obligation to directly comply with the difference principle, though. Directly following a clearer principle, the effects of which overlap with the intended effects of the difference principle (one that promotes equality and is reasonably consistent with efficiency), has advantages I have already discussed.

In summary, G. A. Cohen's second reply to Pogge and J. Cohen supplies intuitive support for the extension of fundamental justice, but it does nothing to support the extension of regulatory justice; that is, it does nothing to support the claim that the difference principle applies directly to the context of personal choice. In the next section, I argue that a distributive regulatory principle modeled on Peter Singer's public standard of assistance would likely be better suited to the personal context than the difference principle is.

6. Regulatory Principles for the Personal Context

In *The Life You Can Save*, Peter Singer acknowledges that the moral principle he famously defends in "Famine Affluence and Morality" is, in a sense, too demanding.[60] Though he continues to maintain that we are morally required to prevent bad occurrences, such as starvation and preventable disease in the Global South, whenever we can do so without giving up anything of comparable moral importance,[61] he also admits that using such a standard to determine whether a person should be blamed for their behavior is likely to have a discouraging effect. Since the principle he defends requires the psychologically prodigious task of giving to the point where one is nearly as impoverished as those one seeks to help (at least in the absence of widespread compliance), blaming those who fall short is likely to discourage many people from trying at all. To address this problem, Singer suggests that praise and blame should be accorded with reference to a more modest standard. More specifically, better-off individuals should be publicly expected to donate a determinate and comparatively small percentage of their income to poverty relief. The percentage they are expected to donate depends on their particular income bracket, and rates are set progressively in order to ensure that those at the bottom end of a higher bracket are not expected to accept a lower net income than those at the upper end of the bracket immediately below them. The following table provides an example of the sort of standard Singer has in mind:[62]

Table 4.1

Yearly Income	*Donation*
65,000–100,000	2.5%
100,001–150,000	2.5% of the first 100,000 and 5% of the remainder
150,001–400,000	2.5% of the first 100,000; 5% of the next 50,000 and 10% of the remainder
400,001–1,000,000	2.5% of the first 100,000; 5% of the next 50,000; 10% of the next 250,000 and 15% of the remainder
Over 1,000,000	2.5% of the first 100,000; 5% of the next 50,000; 10% of the next 250,000; 15% of the next 600,000 and 20% of the remainder

What Singer is after with his public standard is similar to what I am after in my search for a compelling alternative to the difference principle. There are also important differences, though. First, Singer's standard targets global poverty, whereas the standard I am after is concerned with what co-citizens owe to one another. Though questions about what we owe to distant strangers are certainly important, they lie beyond the scope of this book. Second, I do not endorse Singer's distinction between what morality actually requires and what we ought to be publicly supporting. For Singer, demandingness is a problem primarily because of its discouraging psychological effects. According to him, promoting a less demanding standard is a more effective way of encouraging people to give than promoting a more demanding standard. As such, Singer's public standard is an indirect strategy for (partially) implementing the more demanding standard's requirements.[63] By contrast, I think the factors that make an action-guiding standard too demanding also undermine its claim to moral correctness. My worry is not that the difference principle's demandingness will discourage compliance, but rather that said principle does not leave sufficient space for affection, self-interest, loyalty, and so on. An alternative is needed because the difference principle misrepresents what citizens are obligated to do for each other in their daily lives, not because promoting some other principle is a more effective way to implement the difference principle's requirements.

Despite the above differences between Singer and myself, I think his efforts to formulate a standard, the content of which is responsive to the problem of demandingness, provides a useful starting point when thinking about alternatives to Cohen's welfare-inclusive, prerogative-constrained difference principle. Widespread commitment to a standard modeled on Singer's would benefit the worst-off socio-economic group and reduce the size of the inequality between differently talented citizens. What's more, it would provide clear guidance and thus avoid creating any unchosen inequalities in the distribution of regulatory burden. Rather than trying to guess how much is required of them, citizens need only refer to the above table and perform some relatively simple calculations to determine how much they should be donating to the worst-off.

One worry is that Singer's public standard asks too little of talented citizens. Arguably those who are modestly rich ought to give more than just 5 percent or 10 percent of their incomes to the worst-off (I assume the highest brackets in the above table are not applicable, since a society whose institutions conform to Rawls's principles of justice should not have any 'super rich' citizens). Though it may indeed be the case that 5 percent or 10 percent is too low, it is worth noting that Singer's standard is not meant to be static. He is careful to note that what counts as too demanding is socially and culturally relative, and thus that the standard's demands can reasonably be increased insofar as we succeed in cultivating an ethos of giving. One simple and easy way to promote such an ethos is by talking (and perhaps tweeting) about the standard with one's friends, family, co-workers, and so forth. Discussing the standard, one's reasons for following it, and the sense of fulfillment one (hopefully) gets out of giving will encourage others to follow it and also help to normalize the idea that voluntary giving is an important part of leading a morally fulfilling life. Insofar as citizens begin to see giving as one of the personal goals that make life meaningful, rather than as a burdensome moral task in conflict with those personal goals, then the requirements of our standard can be increased without being unreasonably demanding.[64] In fact, our discussion in section 5 suggests that an ethos of giving is perhaps likely to prevail under Rawlsian institutions.

In spite of its virtues, whether a standard modeled on Singer's is the best alternative to a welfare-inclusive, prerogative-constrained difference principle is still an open question. I merely offer Singer's standard as a promising example of how we might make space for affection, self-interest, loyalty, and so on without also compromising clarity.

7. Conclusion

In conclusion, the purpose of this chapter has been to assess Cohen's attack on the basic structure restriction, especially his replies to the problem of demandingness. I argued that it makes sense to include subjective welfare in the metric of fundamental justice and to balance considerations such as affection, self-interest, and loyalty against fundamental justice when applying it to the context of personal choice; but I also argued that these moves become problematic when it is acknowledged that the issue being debated is whether the difference principle—a principle of regulatory justice—extends to personal choice (hence my claim that Cohen equivocates). As Andrew Williams persuasively argues, a welfare-inclusive, prerogative-constrained difference principle is not sufficiently clear to meet Rawls's publicity condition. What's more, it is incapable of providing clear guidance to those who would seek to follow it. Considering that action guidance is a key function of regulatory principles, the latter problem is perhaps especially concerning. Finally, lack of clarity leads to unchosen inequality of burden, as some followers of the difference principle would inadvertently do more than is required of them, and some would do less. As a result, the difference principle is less fair in the personal context than it is in the institutional context. In light of the various problems that attend lack of clarity, I concluded that we have good reason to look for an alternative to Cohen's welfare-inclusive, prerogative-constrained difference principle. Since Peter Singer's public standard of assistance manages to respond to the problem of demandingness without also sacrificing clarity, his work seems like a good place to start in our search for distributive regulatory principles well-suited to the personal context.

Notes

With the exception of section 5, most of this chapter is composed of material from my 2016 article "Cohen's Equivocal Attack on Rawls's Basic Structure Restriction," *Ethical Perspectives* 23 (3): 499–525. I'm grateful to Peeters Publishers for granting me permission to reproduce the article.

1. Cohen (1992). Reprinted with minor revisions as Chapter 1 of Cohen (2008).
2. Cohen (1997). Reprinted with minor revisions as Chapter 3 of Cohen (2008). For recent discussions of Cohen's critique of incentives and the basic structure restriction, see Estlund (1998); Williams (1998); Murphy (1999); Pogge (2000); J. Cohen (2002); Julius (2003); Tan (2004); Scheffler (2006); Titelbaum (2008); Shiffrin (2010); and Schouten (2013).
3. Cohen (2008) pp. 269–72 and Chapter 7. For Rawls's comments on the difference between the concept of justice and conceptions of justice, see Rawls (1971) pp. 5–6. That there is a disagreement between Rawls and Cohen over the concept of justice is something Thomas Scanlon suggested back in 2006. Since then, Cohen's book *Rescuing Justice and Equality* has made this abundantly clear, and authors commenting on it have voiced agreement. See Scanlon (2006) pp. 85–7; Williams (2008) pp. 122–4; Quong (2010) pp. 336–40; Ripstein (2010) pp. 669–87; Tomlin (2010) pp. 228–35 and pp. 240–6; and Tomlin (2012).
4. For my earlier thoughts about the relationship between Cohen's theses, see Johannsen (2013).
5. Though the relationship between fact-dependence and a principle's scope of application is relevant to this chapter, I have discussed that subject at some length elsewhere. Here, I concern myself with the particular details of the debate between Cohen and his opponents, and the manner in which those details relate to the distinction between fundamental values and regulatory principles. For a discussion of the general relationship between fact-dependence and scope of application, see Johannsen (2013) pp. 139–43.
6. See Pogge (2000) pp. 164–6; and J. Cohen (2002).
7. Singer (2010) Chapter 10.
8. Rawls (1971) pp. 75–83.
9. Cohen (2008) pp. 68–9.
10. Cohen (2008) pp. 48–54.
11. Rawls (1971) pp. 453–4.
12. Cohen (2008) pp. 121–2. For an interesting paper exploring the possibility that eventual widespread access to genetic technologies may have positive or negative implications for the cultivation of an egalitarian ethos, see Feeney (2012) esp. pp. 93–8.
13. Rawls (1971) p. 7.
14. Cohen (2008) pp. 124–5. The above exegesis of the 'basic structure objection' and Cohen's critique of incentives appears in Johannsen (2013) p. 136.
15. Rawls (1971) p. 7.
16. Cohen (2008) pp. 134–5.
17. Cohen (2008) pp. 136–7.
18. For an articulation of the demandingness critique, see Pogge (2000) pp. 152–4 and pp. 163–4. For other discussions of this worry, see Van Parijs (1993); Tan (2004); and Titelbaum (2008).
19. Williams (1998).
20. J. Cohen (2002).
21. Cohen (2008) pp. 315–20.
22. Cohen (2008) pp. 128–9.
23. Cohen (2008) pp. 127–8.
24. Cohen (2008) pp. 126–7.
25. Cohen (2008) chapter 7.
26. Cohen (2008) pp. 3–6.
27. Cohen (2008) p. 268 and pp. 306–7. For discussions of the distinction between evaluative claims and normative claims, see Lawford-Smith (2010) pp. 357–61; Gilabert (2011) pp. 55–9; Tomlin (2012) pp. 377–8 and pp. 383–5; and Valentini (2012) pp. 657–8.
28. Cohen (2008) p. 253, pp. 263–8, and pp. 276–86.

29. See, for example, Cohen (2008) pp. 315–30.
30. Cohen (2008) pp. 6–8.
31. Cohen (1989). See also Cohen (2008) p. 7, p. 271, and pp. 300–2.
32. Cohen (2009) p. 37.
33. Cohen (2011).
34. See footnote 18 in the present chapter.
35. Cohen (2008) p. 375.
36. Cohen (2008) pp. 70–2. See also David Estlund's comment about the breadth of Cohen's personal prerogative in Estlund (1998) pp. 101–2. For Cohen's reply, see Cohen (2008) pp. 390–1.
37. The above description of the demandingness objection and Cohen's personal prerogative appears in Johannsen (2013) p. 143.
38. Cohen (2008) pp. 101–9.
39. Cohen (2008) pp. 402–3. It's worth noting that Cohen makes a further qualification in light of the below-discussed issues of clarity and publicity raised by Andrew Williams. In particular, Cohen notes that it is unreasonable to expect citizens to do something when, because of informational barriers, they are unable to tell that the difference principle requires it of them. Though noting as much serves to remove the worry that an ethos of justice requires blaming citizens who fail to fulfill epistemically inaccessible obligations, a number of additional problems attend lack of clarity. I discuss these problems at length throughout the present chapter. For the above-mentioned qualification, see Cohen (2008) p. 371.
40. Williams (1998) p. 238.
41. Williams (1998) p. 239.
42. Williams (1998) pp. 239–40.
43. Cohen (2008) footnote 48 on p. 106.
44. Cohen (1989) pp. 917–9.
45. See Cohen's discussion of publicity in Cohen (2008) pp. 323–7.
46. For his argument against the claim that clarity is a strict constraint on regulatory principles, see Cohen (2008) pp. 351–4.
47. I concede, however, that there are certain cases where clarity is not a virtue; for example, it is probably good, all things being equal, that the norms governing drink buying between friends at the pub are somewhat vague. For his discussion of such cases, see Cohen (2008) pp. 353–4.
48. I owe thanks to Ryan McSheffrey for raising this objection.
49. Hurley (2003) pp. 212–6.
50. Cohen (2008) pp. 403–6.
51. Cohen (2008) p. 276.
52. See Pogge (2000) pp. 164–6; and J. Cohen (2002) pp. 375–80.
53. Pogge (2000) p. 165.
54. J. Cohen (2002) pp. 377–8. For the source upon which J. Cohen draws when discussing consensual and majoritarian institutions, see Lijphart (1999).
55. Cohen (2008) p. 378.
56. Rawls (1971) p. 115.
57. Peter Singer's public standard of assistance is similar to this. See Singer (2010) pp. 151–73.
58. Cohen (2008) p. 378.
59. Cohen's reply focuses specifically on the extrinsically regrettable status of an unmodifiable, inequality-preserving ethos. See Cohen (2008) pp. 379–80.
60. Singer (2010) pp. 151–73.
61. For the original statement of this principle, see Singer (1972) p. 231.
62. The table I have created is similar to one that Singer himself uses. For Singer's table, see page 164 of Singer (2010).
63. Singer (2010) pp. 150–4.
64. Singer (2010) pp. 150–4.

References

Cohen, G.A. 1989. "On the Currency of Egalitarian Justice." *Ethics* 99: 906–44.

Cohen, G.A. 1992. "Incentives, Inequality, and Community." In *The Tanner Lectures on Human Values*. Vol. 13. Ed. Grethe B. Peterson (Salt Lake City: University of Utah Press).

Cohen, G.A. 1997. "Where the Action Is: On the Site of Distributive Justice." *Philosophy and Public Affairs* 26: 3–30.

Cohen, G.A. 2008. *Rescuing Justice and Equality* (Cambridge, MA: Harvard University Press).

Cohen, G.A. 2009. *Why Not Socialism?* (Princeton: Princeton University Press).

Cohen, G.A. 2011. "Fairness and Legitimacy in Justice, and: Does Option Luck Ever Preserve Justice?" In *On the Currency of Egalitarian Justice, and Other Essays in Political Philosophy*. Ed. Michael Otsuka (Princeton: Princeton University Press). Pp. 124–43.

Cohen, Joshua. 2002. "Taking People as They Are?" *Philosophy and Public Affairs* 30: 363–86.

Estlund, David. 1998. "Liberalism, Equality, and Fraternity in Cohen's Critique of Rawls." *The Journal of Political Philosophy* 6: 99–112.

Feeney, Oliver. 2012. "Incentives, Genetics and the Egalitarian Ethos." *Ethical Perspectives* 19: 83–102.

Gilabert, Pablo. 2011. "Feasibility and Socialism." *The Journal of Political Philosophy* 19: 52–63.

Hurley, Susan. 2003. *Justice, Luck, and Knowledge* (Cambridge, MA: Harvard University Press).

Johannsen, Kyle. 2013. "Cohen on Rawls: Personal Choice and the Ideal of Justice." *Social Philosophy Today* 29: 135–49.

Julius, A.J. 2003. "Basic Structure and the Value of Equality." *Philosophy and Public Affairs* 31: 321–55.

Lawford-Smith, Holly. 2010. "Debate: Ideal Theory—A Reply to Valentini." *The Journal of Political Philosophy* 18: 357–68.

Lijphart, Arend. 1999. *Patterns of Democracy: Government Forms and Performance in Thirty-Six Countries* (New Haven: Yale University Press).

Murphy, Liam B. 1999. "Institutions and the Demands of Justice." *Philosophy and Public Affairs* 27: 251–91.

Pogge, Thomas. 2000. "On the Site of Distributive Justice: Reflections on Cohen and Murphy." *Philosophy and Public Affairs* 29: 137–69.

Quong, Jonathan. 2010. "Justice Beyond Equality." *Social Theory and Practice* 36: 315–40.

Rawls, John. 1971. *A Theory of Justice* (Cambridge, MA: Belknap Press).

Ripstein, Arthur. 2010. "Critical Notice on *Rescuing Justice and Equality*." *Canadian Journal of Philosophy* 40: 669–99.

Scanlon, Thomas. 2006. "Justice, Responsibility, and the Demands of Equality." In *The Egalitarian Conscience: Essays in Honour of G.A. Cohen*. Ed. Christine Sypnowich (Oxford: Oxford University Press). Pp. 70–87.

Scheffler, Samuel. 2006. "Is the Basic Structure Basic?" In *The Egalitarian Conscience: Essays in Honor of G.A. Cohen*. Ed. Christine Sypnowich (New York: Oxford University Press). Pp. 102–29.

Schouten, Gina. 2013. "Restricting Justice: Political Interventions in the Home and in the Market." *Philosophy and Public Affairs* 41: 357–88.

Shiffrin, Seanna V. 2010. "Incentives, Motives, and Talents." *Philosophy and Public Affairs* 38: 111–42.

Singer, Peter. 1972. "Famine, Affluence, and Morality." *Philosophy and Public Affairs* 1: 229–43.

Singer, Peter. 2010. *The Life You Can Save* (New York: Random House).

Tan, Kok-Chor. 2004. "Justice and Personal Pursuits." *The Journal of Philosophy* 101: 331–62.

Titelbaum, Michael G. 2008. "What Would a Rawlsian Ethos of Justice Look Like?" *Philosophy and Public Affairs* 36: 289–322.

Tomlin, Patrick. 2010. "Internal Doubts About Cohen's Rescue of Justice." *The Journal of Political Philosophy* 18: 228–47.

Tomlin, Patrick. 2012. "Can I be a Luck Egalitarian and a Rawlsian?" *Ethical Perspectives* 19: 371–97.

Valentini, Laura. 2012. "Ideal vs. Non-ideal Theory: A Conceptual Map." *Philosophy Compass* 7: 654–64.

Van Parijs, Philippe. 1993. "Rawlsians, Christians and Patriots." *European Journal of Philosophy* 1: 309–42.

Williams, Andrew. 1998. "Incentives, Inequality, and Publicity." *Philosophy and Public Affairs* 27: 225–47.

Williams, Andrew. 2008. "Justice, Incentives and Constructivism." *Ratio* 21: 476–93. Reprinted in *Justice, Equality, and Constructivism: Essays on G.A. Cohen's Rescuing Justice and Equality*. Ed. Brian Feltham (Chichester: Wiley-Blackwell, 2009). Pp. 110–126.

5 Narrow Justice

1. Introduction

The primary purpose of Chapters 3 and 4 was to establish the theoretical *significance* of understanding justice as one fundamental, defeasible value among many. I argued that the plausibility of two theses about justice, one a thesis about its content, the other about its scope, depend upon whether justice's narrowness is understood this way. More specifically, in Chapter 3, I argued that if justice is a defeasible value, then luck egalitarianism provides a compelling account of its content, whereas if justice is regulatory, then luck egalitarianism is a poor conception of it. Similarly, in Chapter 4, I argued that understanding justice as a fundamental value entails that it should be accorded some weight in the personal context. However, I also argued that we have good reason to think that the distributive regulatory principles suitable for the personal and institutional contexts are different, and thus that justice, if identified with optimal institutional regulatory principles, should not be extended to the personal realm.

In the present chapter, my goal is to establish the *plausibility* of understanding justice as one fundamental value among many. Put another way, I argue that what I have been calling the 'pluralist' view of justice's narrowness is, in a theoretically important sense, correct, and that what I have been calling the 'contextualist' view is, in the same theoretically important sense, incorrect. More specifically, I argue that only the pluralist view succeeds at conceptually unifying justice and fairness. What's more, I argue that, contrary to how it may seem, understanding justice as a defeasible value does not require giving up the idea that justice is the first virtue of institutions; that is, it does not require giving up its primacy.

In section 2, I address an important challenge to the claim that justice is composed of a single value. According to this challenge, fairness is not the only consideration internal to justice. Preserving justice's primacy requires that various political values be part of it. Thus, justice is not a single, simple value, but rather a complex value composed of a number of other values. Though preserving primacy strikes me as a worthwhile theoretical goal, I do not think that complicating justice is the right way to accomplish it. I argue that understanding fairness as but one of the values internal to justice produces a conceptually confused position, one that, if rendered consistent, collapses into either the pluralist or contextualist view of narrowness.

In section 3, I respond to the worry that the (implicit) dispute between pluralists and contextualists over the conceptual status of justice is merely verbal and thus of little philosophical interest. To deflect this worry, I argue that taking a position on the conceptual correctness of using a word one way instead of another is non-trivial when divergent uses of a word reflect an underlying theoretical disagreement. I indicate that the underlying disagreement between pluralists and contextualists is about whether fairness is best thought of as procedural, and thus prior to narrow justice; or as substantive, and thus co-extensive with narrow justice.

In section 4, I analyze the Rawlsian case for adopting a procedural understanding of fairness. Drawing upon his comments on 'intuitionism,' I argue that an account of procedural fairness is needed because arbitrarily selecting institutional regulatory principles from among the plausible set is inconsistent with the legitimate exercise of state coercion. However, I also argue that specifying the details of our procedural device in a non-arbitrary way requires appealing to a substantive criterion of distributive fairness embedded in our shared political culture. If I am right, then the position I defend succeeds in marrying two seemingly incompatible positions: (a) the view that justice is a defeasible value and (b) the view that it is the 'first virtue of institutions.'

2. Narrow Justice: Simple or Complex?

The basic argument for accepting the pluralist view of narrowness over the contextualist view finds clear expression in G. A. Cohen's *Rescuing Justice and Equality*. There, he argues that justice and institutional regulatory principles must be distinct from each other by virtue of the fact that some of the considerations said principles reflect are distinct from fairness (e.g., considerations of feasibility, efficiency, compassion, etc.).[1] The externality of various considerations to fairness has already been discussed in previous chapters. Consider once more the harshness objection to luck egalitarianism. Though it is indeed *harsh* to let the imprudent bear burdens that they are responsible for having incurred, is it also *unfair* to let them to do so? It does not seem so. Redistributing from those whose genuine choices (choices for which they can properly be held responsible) have been careful and conscientious to those whose genuine choices have not been is certainly *compassionate* when done to alleviate suffering or satisfy basic needs, but it is also unfair to those who have exercised prudence. Fairness and compassion can come into conflict, and though fairness must give way in cases where its pursuit would be excessively harsh, considerations of compassion, though normatively important, are nonetheless external to the content of fairness.[2]

Consider again the leveling-down objection to egalitarianism. Almost no one would endorse implementing distributive equality if it meant that everyone, including those on the bottom end of a currently unequal distribution, would become worse off. According to Cohen, however, the reason for this aversion has nothing to do with fairness and thus nothing to do with justice. Instead, it is about efficiency. On this basis, Cohen claims that Rawls's permission of incentivizing inequalities is also unrelated to fairness. The reason inequalities in social primary goods traceable to natural talents are merely mitigated, rather than fully redressed, is because redressing them allegedly requires leveling down under certain 'real-world' conditions. The content of the difference principle thus reflects a trade-off between considerations of fairness and efficiency, which in turn means that Rawls's principles are not identical with distributive justice.[3] Distributive fairness, and thus distributive justice, though an important normative input for Rawls, is distinct from the principles he endorses.

In response to Cohen's arguments in *Rescuing Justice and Equality*, some philosophers, many of whom agree with much of the view that I defend in Chapter 3, have replied that justice is a more complicated concept than Cohen would have us believe. On the one hand, they agree that luck egalitarianism is plausible on the condition that it be understood as a conception of a particular value, one that is situated within a picture of the moral universe that includes a plurality of other important values.[4] On the other hand, these theorists reject the view that justice is internally simple. They think that distributive equality is a part of justice but not the whole of it. For example, Jonathan Quong insists that justice is action guiding and that its capacity for action guidance is contingent upon its being a 'complex value,' that is, a value whose content reflects a wide variety of normative considerations.[5] He correctly notes that principles that do not take into account a wide variety of considerations cannot plausibly serve as criteria for determining what political actions to take, all things considered.[6] Similarly Pablo Gilabert, in his discussion of Cohen's *Why Not Socialism?*, suggests that justice is best thought of as being constituted by a plurality of reasons that must be weighed against each one another when determining what our duties of justice are. Instead of thinking of compromises between luck equality and, say, community, as a compromise between justice and community, Gilabert recommends that we instead think of them as compromises between two different considerations of justice that must be weighed against each other when determining what justice itself requires. The alternative is to think of justice as a 'non-trumping value,' and Gilabert finds that implausible.[7]

It is noteworthy that Gilabert and Quong do not equate luck egalitarianism with fairness. Quong, for example, seems more inclined towards the Rawlsian view of fairness that I will be discussing shortly.[8] Despite this, many of the philosophers who understand luck egalitarianism as part of but not the entirety of distributive justice explicitly identify it as the fairness element of justice, namely Shlomi Segall, Adam Swift, and Patrick Tomlin.[9] It is specifically their understanding of the relationship between luck equality, fairness, and justice that I will henceforth be addressing.[10]

The distinction between broad and narrow justice poses a serious problem for the view that a plurality of values, fairness included, are internal to justice. As the reader may recall, Aristotle begins his discussion of justice in *The*

Nicomachean Ethics by distinguishing between two different but related senses of the term: a narrow sense of the word 'justice' that refers to a part of morality, specifically the part pertaining to fairness, and which bears on matters of distribution and rectification, and a broader sense of the word 'justice' that refers to moral rightness in general.[11] Though I think it is sensible to assume that in most cases political philosophers employ the narrow sense of the term 'justice,' let's drop that assumption and inquire into which sense of the word is intended by proponents of the view that fairness is but one of the values internal to justice.

Suppose the above view is meant to pertain to narrow justice. If so, then it makes no sense. If the view that fairness is but one of the values internal to 'justice' is a view about specifically 'narrow justice,' then it is the view that fairness is a part of fairness. Assuming that a part of something is always to be contrasted with the whole of it, the claim that fairness is a part of fairness is analytically false. Instead, suppose that the view under analysis is a view about broad justice. If this is the way it is interpreted, then it is equivalent to the view that fairness is but one of the considerations that must be taken into account when determining what, all things considered, is the right course of action. A broad interpretation of the view has the virtue of not producing an analytically false position. Unfortunately, however, it also has the vice of being trivially true, at least for any value pluralist who thinks of fairness as a value that can come into conflict with other important values. It is obvious that fairness, as one value among others, has only ceteris paribus normative force. Determining the correct all-thing-considered action of course requires taking other normative factors into consideration, factors that will often require striking a compromise. If those who think of 'justice' as complex merely mean to draw attention to fairness's ceteris paribus normative status, then their position is not really an alternative to the pluralist view of narrowness. After all, pluralists also think that fairness should be compromised for the sake of other values. It is just that those who think of 'justice' as complex, if using the term in its broad sense, are referring to a different concept.

On the assumption that those who identify justice as a complex value are not just talking about broad justice, I think the source of confusion for at least some of them is an uncritical marriage between two views. The first is the pluralist view that narrow justice is a value that sometimes conflicts with other values. The second is the ostensibly contextualist, Rawlsian view that narrow justice is the most significant normative consideration in matters of institutional design. In Rawls's words: "Justice is the first virtue of social institutions, as truth is of systems of thought. A theory however elegant and economical must be rejected or revised if it is untrue; likewise laws and institutions no matter how efficient and well-arranged must be reformed or abolished if they are unjust."[12] It is because these theorists embrace the first view that it is plausible to think they are talking about the same thing as those who hold the pluralist view of narrowness, namely about which considerations are internal and which are external to a particular value. It is because they think of justice as 'the first virtue of institutions,' however, that they find themselves pushed towards the view that considerations of more than just fairness are internal. To say that justice is the first virtue is to say that a society's institutions must be just in order to be acceptable. It ostensibly follows that for a normative requirement to be a requirement of justice, it must possess a considerable amount of weight in the institutional context. A straightforward way to try and account for this weight is by interpreting justice to be a value whose content reflects a plurality of normative considerations. If the requirements of justice are interpreted as the output of practical political deliberation, rather than as a defeasible input to be balanced against other defeasible inputs, then justice can reasonably be accorded the kind of weight it seemingly needs to have in order to be the first virtue. The problem, however, is that these views are in tension with each other. They embody different understandings of justice's narrowness and thus different understandings of the way fairness works in matters of distribution.

On the first understanding of narrow justice, fairness is a value that sometimes conflicts with other values. As I argue in Chapter 3, luck egalitarianism supplies the best conception of this value, and problems such as those posed by the harshness objection represent constraints on the extent to which fairness can permissibly be implemented in practice, rather than problems that require amending the content of our conception of fairness. The problem holding this view poses, as we have already noted, is that, on this understanding, fairness and narrow justice are the same thing. It makes no sense to say that fairness is a part of narrow justice.

In the second understanding of narrow justice, fairness operates somewhat differently. It operates as a procedure for rationally determining which institutional regulatory principles accord correct weights to our conflicting values. In Rawls's critical discussion of 'intuitionism' (value pluralism),[13] he claims that it is not acceptable to arbitrarily select a society's institutional regulatory principles from among the set of plausible alternatives. He sees it as a serious failure of value pluralism that it is to some extent indeterminate between alternatives. Any adequate theory of justice must, in his view, make use of a criterion that non-arbitrarily identifies particular regulatory principles as the best. His own solution to what one might call 'the problem of arbitrariness' is the original position. Via this device, Rawls attempts rationally to select institutional principles from among the plausible set that despite reflecting a variety of normative considerations are nonetheless entirely fair by virtue of having been chosen through a fair procedure.[14]

The second understanding of fairness, unlike the first one we discussed, can make sense of the idea that fairness is a part of narrow justice. On this view, fairness and justice are related but not identical. Instead of saying fairness is justice, it would be more accurate to say that fairness is prior to justice.[15] Procedural fairness is the part of a theory of narrow justice that we employ to select its principles. The problem holding this view poses, however, is that it no longer makes sense to think of fairness as conflicting with other values. Procedural fairness is not one of the defeasible values that our regulatory principles must partially live up to. Instead, it is the means via which one chooses from among the plausible set of regulatory alternatives. It is for this reason that Rawls's theory is appropriately thought of as a theory of specifically narrow justice. Understanding fairness procedurally, rather than as a value subject to trade-offs, makes it reasonable to predicate full fairness of his regulatory principles and thus to consider them as principles that tell us what justice *is* (as opposed to a theory of what justice requires of us once all other things have been taken into consideration). In Rawls's view, principles that, for example, allow some to receive a greater share of society's resources on the basis of morally arbitrary natural talents or that compensate those who are poorly off due to voluntary expensive tastes are still entirely fair if selected via a fair procedure.

So those who hold the position that fairness is one among a plurality of values internal to justice are stuck between a rock and a hard place. On the one hand, they can keep the view that narrow justice is a value and concede that fairness *is* narrow justice, and thus that it is only a part of all-things-considered rightness. Were they to do so, then their view would just collapse into the pluralist view of narrowness; they would hold that narrow justice is a fundamental value that is co-extensive with fairness. Alternatively, they can keep the view that narrow justice is a 'complex value' but give up the view that fairness is a substantive, defeasible value that luck egalitarianism plausibly captures the content of. If narrow justice is complex, then fairness needs to be understood procedurally, for only then can a principle that reflects a plurality of considerations be plausibly thought of as fully fair and thus as a principle of what justice *is*. Principles that embody a compromise between luck egalitarian fairness and the values with which it conflicts cannot be thought to possess complete fairness and thus can only be thought to convey what narrow justice requires of us once all other things have been taken into consideration.

In my own view, marrying the idea that justice is a value to the idea that it is also the first virtue of institutions is a worthy theoretical goal. However, I do not think interpreting it as a complex value is the right way to achieve that goal. Instead, the approach I will take is to argue that luck egalitarian fairness has two roles to play with respect to the selection of institutional regulatory principles. On the one hand, I will maintain that it is a defeasible value that must be accorded at least some weight by any of the plausible regulatory alternatives from among which a choice is to be made. On the other, I will argue that it has an important role to play at the procedural level too, and that it is by virtue of its procedural role that luck egalitarianism is appropriately considered the 'first virtue of institutions.' This thought will be discussed at greater length in section 4. For the moment, however, I turn to a fresh issue, namely the concern that the dispute between Cohen and Rawls over justice's narrowness is merely verbal.

3. Cohen vs. Rawls on the Concept of Justice: A Merely Verbal Dispute?

The purpose of the present section is to address two problems. The first is the above-mentioned worry that the dispute between pluralists and contextualists over the conceptual status of justice is merely semantic and thus not of any philosophical interest. The second is Ronald Dworkin's claim that the concept of justice is 'abstract equality' and that any plausible conception of abstract equality is both a full, uncompromised theory of justice *and* an indefeasible standard in light of which institutions should be designed. Aside from the fact that both pose challenges for the pluralist position, the first and second issues are related because addressing them will involve an exploration of the different ways in which an understanding of a concept can be 'correct.'

Non-trivially establishing that one understanding of a concept is better than another is tricky. It is a truism that the meaning of a word is determined by convention. As a result, a word whose standard use involves a particular meaning at present can easily lose that meaning in the future. For instance, in contemporary English the word 'cause' is almost always used in its efficient sense. If someone says 'X causes Y,' she probably means that X either brings about or contributes to bringing about the occurrence of Y. The ancient Greeks, in contrast, associated 'cause' with a number of different meanings. Though they sometimes had the efficient sense in mind, often the word was used in other ways, such as to refer to something's material composition. To say that X causes Y in this sense is to say that X is what Y is made of. When used in these different ways, the word 'cause' reflects two very distinct concepts. Though retaining both uses will sometimes make it necessary to disambiguate how the term is being used, there is nothing particularly amiss with sometimes using the word one way and sometimes using it the other, and thus nothing peculiar about claiming that *both* uses are correct. Of course, it is possible that a dispute could nonetheless emerge over the proper use of the word. The disputants might perhaps disagree over which use of the word is consistent with contemporary linguistic convention (in which case the champion of its efficient sense would be correct). Such a dispute would be merely linguistic, however, and thus of little interest to philosophers.

On one interpretation, then, the disagreement over justice's narrowness is merely a linguistic one and thus does not constitute a substantive issue. For Rawls and other liberals who hold a contextual view of narrowness, optimal institutional regulatory principles are identical with what 'justice' is. In contrast, for Cohen and other value pluralists who understand 'justice' to be a fundamental value, institutional regulatory principles specifically tells us what we should do, all things, including 'justice,' considered. Pluralists maintain that, properly speaking, 'justice' is fairness, and thus only a conception of the content of distributive fairness is a conception of the content of distributive 'justice.' But isn't this just a verbal dispute? Would we lose anything by dropping the term 'justice' altogether?[16]

In some verbal disagreements, it is not right to say that the nature of the dispute is *merely* linguistic. Sometimes divergent uses of a word reflect a theoretical disagreement, one that manifests itself linguistically but is deeper than a dispute over standard usage. Moral theorists' use of the word 'morality' is arguably a good example of this. For most moral theorists, a conception of morality is a conception of right action. Proponents of different conceptions, such as utilitarians and deontologists, disagree over the principles that spell out morality's content, but they implicitly agree that the concept of 'morality' is to be understood as 'right action.' The proponents of virtue ethics are ostensibly an exception to this. For virtue ethicists, a conception of morality is a conception of virtuous character. Different virtue ethicists sometimes disagree about how particular virtues should be understood or about the relationship between them, but they implicitly agree that the concept of morality is to be understood in terms of the virtues that constitute a virtuous character. To treat these different uses of the term 'morality' as merely a verbal disagreement is to miss that they reflect a significant theoretical disagreement. Virtue ethicists and other moral theorists disagree over how the relationship between character and action should be understood. For the virtue ethicist, right action can only be understood with reference to an account of moral character. Right actions are those that flow from virtue, and thus identifying them presupposes an account of the virtues. Other theorists, in contrast, see moral character as parasitic upon right action. For them, the value of a character trait depends upon the value of the actions it is conducive to, making an account of right action more fundamental than an account of moral character.[17]

The above considerations suggest that offering a non-trivial defense of the claim that justice is a fundamental value requires demonstrating two things: (1) that divergent uses of the term 'justice' reflect a theoretical disagreement, and (2) that the pluralist view is on the correct side of that disagreement. Accomplishing these tasks is the purpose of my next section. As I have already suggested in the previous section, the pluralist understanding of narrow justice and the contextualist understanding differ with respect to the way fairness is construed. In the pluralist understanding, fairness is substantive, and the term justice, understood in its narrow sense, is just another word for it. This understanding of justice entails that to provide a theory of what justice *is* requires supplying the evaluative principle that we think best specifies the content of distributive fairness, such as the principle of luck equality. In the contextualist view, however, a theory of narrow justice is not the same thing as a theory of fairness. Justice is of course substantive, but fairness is not. Here is a helpful quote from Rawls:

> The original position is, one might say, the appropriate initial status quo, and thus the fundamental agreements reached within it are fair. This explains the propriety of the name "justice as fairness": it conveys the idea that the principles of justice are agreed to in an initial situation that is fair. The name does not mean that the concepts of justice and fairness are the same, any more than the phrase "poetry as metaphor" means that the concepts of poetry and metaphor are the same.[18]

It is a procedural understanding of fairness that licenses contextualists like Rawls to locate the concept of narrow justice at the level of institutional regulatory principles; that is, it licenses them to say that institutional regulatory principles express what justice *is*, not just what is required of us, all things, including justice, considered. In light of this, I submit that an implicit disagreement about the nature of fairness underlies the pluralist and contextualist understandings of narrowness. It is to that disagreement that I turn in the next section. Before I do so, however, I would like to explain a second kind of non-trivial argument for the correctness of a concept. The pertinence of this kind of argument to a defense of the pluralist understanding of narrowness will become apparent when I get to the particular example I am going to use, namely the idea that 'abstract equality' unites contemporary theories of justice.[19]

The second kind of non-trivial argument for the correctness of a concept is, in a sense, the opposite of the first kind. Whereas the first kind involves identifying the theoretical disagreement that explains two different uses of a word, the second kind involves identifying that which disagreeing theorists implicitly agree about and which thus unites their differing theories. When one's goal is to identify that which unites competing theories, saying that a particular sense of a word is the 'correct' sense is the same as saying that it is the sense theorists are actually talking about and attempting to interpret.[20] Though arguments of this sort are similar to arguments that claim a particular way of using a word is more consistent with standard usage than another, the reason they are non-trivial is because they have implications for the way competing theories are to be understood and assessed. For example, when comparing the merits of the principle of average utility to Rawls's theory, it makes a difference whether we understand them to be competing conceptions of institutional rightness or competing conceptions of comprehensive morality. Though Rawls's two principles arguably have various theoretical advantages over the principle of average utility, at least some of those advantages dissolve when his principles are thought to be regulative of not only the institutional context, but the personal context as well. A version of the difference principle that possesses all-things-considered normative force within the realm of personal choice, and is thus not constrained by a personal prerogative, would be extremely demanding. As was mentioned in Chapter 4, such a principle would require that in any set of circumstances where a potential choice is likely to benefit the least well-off more than its alternatives, members of society will be required to consistently make that choice in spite of their personal preferences. Interpreted this way, Rawls's theory might not fare much better than the principle of average utility would.

A great example of this second sort of concept argument is Ronald Dworkin's 'egalitarian plateau.' According to Dworkin, contemporary theories of justice are united in their efforts to interpret the same concept, namely 'abstract equality.' As is often the case with concepts, characterizing the concept of abstract equality in a way that does not presuppose any particular conception of it is perhaps a bit tricky, but Dworkin and others have suggested a number of characterizations that arguably work. In *Contemporary Political Philosophy*, Will Kymlicka writes: "A theory is egalitarian in this sense if it accepts that the interests of each member of the community matter, and matter equally."[21] In *Sovereign Virtue*, Dworkin himself writes: "No government is legitimate that does not show equal concern for the fate of all those citizens over whom it claims dominion and from whom it claims allegiance."[22] The claim that an abstract version of equality underlies even inegalitarian theories of justice may seem implausible at first blush, but Kymlicka has given the idea a fair amount of credence in his analyses of the various theories of justice covered in *Contemporary Political Philosophy*. For example, it might initially seem implausible to think of utilitarian theories of justice as interpretations of equality. As we noted in Chapter 2, however, utilitarianism, or at least maximum average utilitarianism, contains within it the egalitarian thesis that each member of the political community's welfare is to be accorded equal weight when being promoted. Though equal weight is not a form of distributive equality, it is nonetheless an interpretation of a more abstract idea of equality,[23] and this abstract idea should arguably be associated with other contemporary theories of justice as well.

With respect to his own luck egalitarian theory of justice, Dworkin uses the idea of abstract equality to accomplish at least a couple of noteworthy theoretical functions. One was already discussed in Chapter 3. There, we considered the possibility of interpreting the ideal of an ambition-sensitive, endowment-insensitive distribution to be Dworkin's defeasible principle of luck egalitarian justice, and his insurance market device, in turn, to be his conception of all-things-considered institutional rightness. However, we also noted that such an interpretation is contrary to Dworkin's own understanding of his theory. According to Dworkin, the hypothetical insurance market is not a pragmatic compromise. Though it is indeed responsive to facts about the real world, it nonetheless fully represents justice in his view because it is an interpretation of abstract equality.[24] Abstract equality thus allows Dworkin to say that the hypothetical insurance market is a theory of what justice *is*, despite the fact that it deviates somewhat from full luck equality.

In addition to allowing him to say that the hypothetical insurance market is a full theory of justice, the idea of abstract equality is also used as a resource when explaining why the hypothetical insurance market is a necessary part of his theory. For example, when responding to the worry that his theory unpalatably implies we should level down, Dworkin notes that one of the functions of moving from an ambition-sensitive, endowment-insensitive distribution to the hypothetical insurance market is to avoid this consequence, for it would indeed be problematic if there were no cut-off point at which those with very costly illnesses or disabilities cease to be compensated. Furthermore, he notes that avoiding levelling down is important precisely because no plausible interpretation of abstract equality would permit it. A government that completely impoverishes its citizens in a futile effort to fully compensate all forms of bad brute luck is not showing equal concern for their fates, and any theory of justice that would require as much can therefore be rejected on egalitarian grounds, according to Dworkin.[25]

What, then, are we to make of the idea of abstract equality and Dworkin's use of it? Is Dworkin right to say that abstract equality rules out any theory of justice that requires levelling down? And is he right to say that interpretations of it fashioned for real-world circumstances are full, uncompromised theories of justice? Addressing these questions is important, for they seem to threaten the pluralist understanding of narrow justice, as well as the conception of it that I defend. After all, when justice is understood as a defeasible value that must be compromised in practice, the upshot is that any theory of all-things-considered institutional rightness is considered a morally necessary departure from justice, not an interpretation of it. Furthermore, though defeasible luck equality does not strictly speaking *require* levelling down, as it can be traded off against the competing demands of efficiency, it does nonetheless provide an ineliminable *reason* to level down, as permitting inequality for the sake of efficiency is considered a regrettable departure from fairness. If Dworkin's right, though, and all plausible theories of justice are interpretations of abstract equality, then a defeasible theory of justice is, in a sense, just as bad as one that would require levelling down. Why? Because a defeasible interpretation deprives abstract equality of its status as the 'sovereign virtue.' This problem should seem familiar. In the last section, we noted that a concern for preserving justice's status as the 'first virtue of institutions' was motivating the idea that justice is best thought of as a complex value.

In order to see whether the above worries have any bite, an analysis of the idea of abstract equality is called for. As I noted earlier, one possibility is to think of abstract equality as the claim that each member of the community's interests matter equally. Another possibility is to think of it as equal concern for the fate of citizens. Regardless of the particular wording we use, the value concepts employed are the same. First, there is the idea of citizens' *fate* or *interests*. Second, there is the idea that the interests of citizens *matter* or are appropriate objects of *concern*. Third, there is the idea that the interests of citizens matter *equally*. We have three concepts, then. *Equality*, *concern*, and *interests*. The concept of *interests* is fairly straightforward. It is just another word for citizens' good.[26] Furthermore, for a government to be *concerned* for citizen's interests is to say that the realization of their good matters to it, that is, that it, in some sense, cares whether citizens successfully achieve their good. Though it is possible that some ways of understanding concern come apart from the concept of efficiency, that is, come apart from the idea of increasing the total amount, concern for the realization of citizens' good and the efficient promotion of their good are certainly similar concepts. The main difference, I think, is that the concept of concern is somewhat more specific. Concern is specifically concern for 'the good' of people and thus for the amount of the 'the good' that they enjoy, rather than for increasing the amount of 'the good' in general. This seems to rule out the possibility of understanding 'concern' in an aggregative fashion, since an aggregative understanding ostensibly requires that we sacrifice people's good for the sake of increasing the total amount of 'the good' through population growth.[27] As I indicated in Chapter 2, aggregative interpretations of efficiency strike me as implausible for precisely this sort of reason. Based on the assumption that most other political philosophers share my intuition, I am willing to accept the claim that efficiency, when applied to 'the good', is only of common interest to political philosophers insofar as one has in mind the efficient promotion of people's good, rather than the efficient promotion of 'the good' in general.

Finally, the idea that a government should not only be concerned for the realization of its citizens' good but *equally* concerned for all citizens suggests that a standard of fairness must constrain the manner in which governments go about realizing their citizens' good. Governments cannot just go about ignoring the good of some and promoting the good of others; they must promote citizens' good in a way that is fair, or to be more specific, in a way that is equal.

If the above understanding of the concept of abstract equality is correct, then abstract equality is a *complex value* made up of three concepts, namely equality, concern, and the good. Furthermore, if Dworkin is correct to say that abstract equality serves as an 'egalitarian plateau' in contemporary political theory, then it is the complex value that contemporary political philosophers are referring to when they use the term 'justice.' Perhaps Dworkin is right about abstract equality. Though it strikes me that Rawls's conception of justice in particular is operating with various other value concepts too (e.g., fraternity (community), publicity, etc.), perhaps some of those values are not common to all of the literature and should thus be omitted from our characterization of the concept that allegedly captures what everyone is talking about. If there is one thing that comes out quite clearly in the previous section, however, it is that in the pluralist picture of justice's narrowness, a picture shared by philosophers such as Isaiah Berlin, Joel Feinberg, and (for the most part) G. A. Cohen, justice is not a complex value. It is one fundamental, irreducible value among a plurality of irreducible values, rather than a composite of values. As such, the concept underlying their use of the term 'justice' is not the concept of abstract equality. In all likelihood, it is instead one of the concepts that partially makes up the concept of abstract equality, specifically the standard of fairness that constrains the manner in which a government may show concern for its citizens' good.

An upshot of the above is that the pluralist use of the word 'justice' is arguably at odds with much (but not all) of the contemporary literature. However, this does not necessarily mean that one is wrong to use it that way. As I noted earlier in this section, there is more than one way to non-trivially argue for the correctness of a concept. Though there is a sense in which a particular way of using a word is correct if it accurately captures what theorists are talking about, there is another sense that is not contingent upon linguistic usage. A particular way of using a word can be correct in this second sense if (a) there is a theoretical disagreement underlying divergent uses of the word, and (b) the particular way of using it in question is on the correct side of that disagreement. And as I have already argued, I think the crux of the disagreement between those who use the word 'justice' to refer to a defeasible value and those who use it in its complex or regulatory sense lies in the way in which they understand the fairness part of institutional rightness. Rawls, as we have already noted, has an explicitly procedural understanding of fairness. The principles a society adopts for purposes of regulating the design of institutions are fair, in his view, as are any distributive inequalities subsequently produced, so long as those principles would hypothetically be adopted in the original position. Similarly Dworkin, as we have already noted, employs a procedural understanding of fairness when he employs his hypothetical insurance device. In his view, the manner in which institutions distribute resources is fair so long as any inequalities traceable to brute luck are consistent with the insurance packages citizens would hypothetically purchase. Pluralists like Cohen, in stark contrast, see any inequality traceable to brute luck as unfair, full stop. Procedural devices like the original position and hypothetical insurance market may or may not be fruitful approaches to institutional regulation, but even if they are, they do not have the power to transform a seemingly unfair inequality into a fair one, and thus they do not have the capacity to confer full, uncompromised justice upon either a distribution or a set of distributive principles. Cohen thinks that fairness is the right understanding of distributive equality, and if this means justice must be understood as a defeasible value, one that conflicts with and thus must be balanced against concern and other values, rather than as the 'sovereign' output of that balancing act, then so be it.[28]

In the next section, I address the procedural versus substantive fairness divide that separates the pluralist understanding of justice's narrowness from the contextualist understanding of narrowness we find in Rawls and Dworkin. Though I focus on Rawls's work in particular, I take his reasons for adopting a procedural interpretation of fairness to be more or less representative of the contextualist position in general (a fair assumption, I hope, given Rawls's unparalleled impact on contemporary political philosophy). While I am sympathetic to the concerns that I think motivate Rawls, I also think that choosing to replace a substantive understanding of fairness with a procedural understanding reflects a failure to appreciate the full scope of the problem that makes a procedural interpretation necessary in the first place. What's more, I will argue that there is an important sense in which fairness can be both a defeasible value *and* the first virtue of institutions.

4. Fairness and Legitimacy

(a) The Problem of Arbitrariness

In his discussion of the view he calls 'intuitionism' (a term he uses to refer to value pluralism),[29] Rawls considers a way of understanding justice that, at least on the face of it, looks rather like the pluralist understanding. More specifically, he considers the possibility that the way we should go about deciding how to order our society's institutions is by striking a balance between a plurality of competing principles, one of which is an egalitarian principle of justice or fairness.[30] Though Rawls acknowledges that intuitionistic balancing is not an irrational approach, he also indicates that we should hope for more. While weightings that drastically favor one desiderata over another can be ruled out as implausible, such as a weighting that accords great significance to justice but only minimal significance to efficiency (or vice versa), intuitionistic balancing provides no standard in light of which to decide between trade-off packages that fall along a moderate spectrum. Rawls does not dwell long upon why he finds this problematic, but he does mention that the choice of trade-off packages is not insignificant. Quite the contrary, citizens may deeply disagree over how competing desiderata should be weighted, and when they do, they are far from indifferent towards the choice of weightings made by the state.[31] What's more, the choice of weightings is something different citizens have a personal stake in. For example, when deciding the appropriate trade-off point between efficiency and justice, it makes a difference to different citizens whether a more efficiency-heavy or justice-heavy trade-off point is selected. For those who lack economically productive talents, a more justice-heavy trade-off point could make a significant difference to how well their lives end up going. For those who possess economically productive talents and could potentially benefit from incentives, it makes a difference whether the trade-off point selected permits them to keep a larger share rather than a smaller share of the additional wealth their talents generate. The thought then seems to be that a fair way of adjudicating between the different trade-off packages populating the plausible set is necessary and, though Rawls does not explicitly say it, that we therefore need a procedural understanding of fairness. Ostensibly a principle of fairness that is itself one of the principles being traded off cannot help to fairly decide between trade-off packages, and so a different understanding of fairness that can serve this function is called for.

But why is it so important to have a fair way of adjudicating between trade-off packages? What would be wrong with arbitrarily selecting a particular package and saying "Tough luck!" to those who would have preferred a different one? The answer, I think, lies in the familiar liberal idea that state coercion needs to be justifiable to those who are coerced. After all, the function of the particular trade-off package selected will be to serve as the guide in light of which a society's set of institutions, many of which are *coercively imposed*, will be designed. If the choice between plausible trade-off packages is an arbitrary one, how can that choice be justified to citizens? Intuitionism provides the moral resources needed to determine what the plausible set of trade off packages is and thus offers a basis upon which to justify restricting the range of options from which to choose, but it seemingly does not supply the resources needed to justify choosing one particular package over another. It provides us with nothing to say to the talented individual who claims that a tax scheme that provides her with a somewhat larger allotment of incentives is equally justified on grounds of efficiency, or, in the event that a more efficiency-heavy package is adopted, nothing to say to the untalented individual who complains that further taxing the talented is equally justified on grounds of justice.[32]

If the above analysis is correct, then what is at stake between the pluralist's understanding of fairness as one value among a plurality of values and a procedural understanding of fairness is the possibility of legitimately using institutional regulatory principles as a basis for coercion. The worry is that arbitrarily choosing from among the set of plausible all-things-considered options is inconsistent with justified coercion, and thus that understanding fairness as one of the values to be traded off is the wrong approach. Instead, only a procedural understanding of fairness provides us with the resources needed to non-arbitrarily make a choice.

The original position is not Rawls's only method for tackling trade-offs. His other method is to assign lexical priorities.[33] Since liberties take priority over all else in his theory, a lesser degree of liberty cannot be justified by an increase in opportunities or material goods such as wealth and income (except in circumstances of abject scarcity). Similarly, since opportunities take priority over material goods, an increase in the latter cannot justify a decrease in the former. Lexically prioritizing different goods is thus one way to adjudicate between them in cases of conflict. Lexical prioritizing is an incomplete solution, however. For one, there is a question about why the particular order decided upon is justified. Answering this question is one of the original position's functions.[34] Furthermore, Rawls's lexical ordering only addresses a sub-set of trade-offs: specifically trade-offs between goods. Another kind of trade-off must be made between what might be called 'functions', that is, concepts that tell us what to do with goods (and possibly other metrics).[35] Equality and efficiency are concepts like this. Equality directs us to distribute goods equally. Efficiency, by contrast, directs us to increase the (aggregate or average) amount of goods (possibly to the point where no one can further benefit without someone else suffering a loss). Insofar as these goals are in tension, however, we need some way to balance them against each other. Assigning one lexical priority over the other does not work in this case, as it is not plausible to completely sacrifice equality for efficiency or vice versa. Instead, what is needed is a non-arbitrary method for selecting a regulatory principle that specifies a legitimately enforceable trade-off point between them, such as the difference principle. Under the difference principle, inequalities necessary to produce a larger aggregate or average amount of social primary goods are permitted on the condition that they maximally benefit the worst-off. Since a larger inequality that increases the amount of primary goods but does not further benefit the worst-off is impermissible, the difference principle specifies the point at which equality may no longer be sacrificed for efficiency. What's more, it does so in a way that can be justified to citizens: we can tell them that they would hypothetically agree to the difference principle under the veil of ignorance because it assures them that any relative disadvantages they may be forced to endure will work to their absolute benefit. We will further discuss the interpersonal justification for the difference principle in the next sub-section.

(b) The Role of Reasonableness in Specifying a Fair Contract Situation

In the previous sub-section, I explained that the function of procedural fairness is to provide a fair way of adjudicating between conflicting values. Given that different people weigh political values in different yet equally reasonable ways, a fair way of selecting principles that reflect particular weightings is necessary. Unless the state can justify its particular choice of weightings to those who may reasonably disagree, it cannot legitimately enforce that choice.

Given that the function of a procedural interpretation of fairness is to solve what I will call 'the problem of arbitrariness,' it is natural to wonder whether it succeeds in doing so. Does Rawls's original position actually provide a non-arbitrary basis upon which to decide between the regulatory options populating the plausible set? Though it certainly provides a basis upon which to select a particular regulatory option, that basis is non-arbitrary only if there is good reason to use it and not some other basis. As Rawls himself notes, more than a single description of the original position is possible. More information could be allowed past the veil of ignorance, the psychological description of the contracting parties could be altered somewhat, and so on. What's more, the details of the particular description one opts for can potentially affect the choice of principles it would be rational for contracting parties to agree to.[36] It arguably would not be rational for everyone to agree to a principle that maximally benefits the least well-off if the parties knew something about the talents they possess and thus about the likelihood that their skills will be in high demand. Given that various descriptions of the original position are possible, it is important that the particular description we decide upon is itself selected on a non-arbitrary basis. Otherwise we would just be pushing the problem from the level of regulatory principle adoption up to the level of procedure selection.

So what underlies Rawls's description of the original position? One possible answer can be found in his post–*A Theory of Justice* discussion in *Political Liberalism*.[37] There, Rawls indicates that the original position is a "device of representation" intended to model the conditions under which fair terms of cooperation would be adopted for a society understood as a "fair system of cooperation between free and equal citizens."[38] Given his understanding of the function of the original position, it might be thought that the ideas composing Rawls's understanding of society are the basis upon which the particular details of the original position are justified. I think this is true to some extent. Consider his political conception of the person, for example. For persons to be free and equal in the Rawlsian sense of these terms is more or less to say that they are able to reason about, formulate a conception of, and subsequently pursue what they take to be the good (hence the predicate 'free'); that they are able to understand and follow their society's principles of justice, albeit indirectly via an institutionally focused 'natural duty of justice';[39] and that they are all able to perform the aforementioned tasks to the extent necessary to fully participate in the economic, social, and political life of their society (hence the predicate 'equal').[40] With this conception of the person in mind, a conception that Rawls claims is embedded in our shared democratic political culture, some features of the original position seem to straightforwardly follow. Rough equality with respect to their capacity to function as members in their society suggests that, among other things, contracting parties in the original position should all have an equal say over which principles are adopted. But what constitutes having an equal say? It is not obvious that the idea of citizens as full participants in society means that they should be deprived of all information regarding their class background or talents. These are an important part of anyone's identity, after all, so why shouldn't the parties have this information?[41]

I suggest that, like Rawls, we look to the contents of our shared democratic political culture for answers. More specifically, if there is an idea of fairness embedded in our political culture that can function to identify which aspects of the parties' identities would, if included in the original position, make it an unfair contract situation, then we would have a clear answer to the arbitrariness problem. What's more, the fact that the idea of fairness employed is drawn from among the ideas embedded in our shared political culture performs an important function; its place there means that it is a ground that we can reasonably expect our fellow citizens to accept. Only reasonable grounds are suitable resources to draw upon when resolving the problem of arbitrariness. If we cannot reasonably expect citizens to accept our reasons for describing the original position a certain way, then we will be unable to interpersonally justify the regulatory principles selected. And if we are unable to interpersonally justify our regulatory principles, that is, if we are unable to justify our regulatory principles to citizens who will live under the coercive institutions those principles regulate, then we will have failed to achieve legitimacy.[42]

It might be thought that the idea that motivates looking within our shared political culture, that is, the idea of reasonableness, is itself sufficient to account for why fairness requires placing knowledge of social positions and natural talents behind the veil of ignorance. In fact, Rawls explicitly notes that the function of the veil of ignorance is to situate rational agents so that their deliberations are subject to certain conditions, namely the conditions that must be met in order for their subsequent agreement to be reasonable.[43] A closer look at the idea of reasonableness is warranted for this reason.

In *Political Liberalism*, Rawls explains that reasonableness is part of an idea of fairness central to his theory of justice: the idea of reciprocity. Reciprocity, as he understands it, is a relationship between citizens.[44] One of the requirements it imposes is that all those engaged in cooperation "benefit in an appropriate way as assessed by a suitable benchmark of comparison."[45] Another requirement, however, is that the principles that regulate shared institutions be reasonably acceptable to all cooperators. In other words, reciprocity is a combination of the ideas of mutual acceptability and mutual benefit.[46]

In the "The Idea of Public Reason Revisited," Rawls suggests that it is antithetical to reasonableness, and thus to reciprocity, for someone to accept terms of cooperation because they are "dominated or manipulated, or under the pressure of an inferior social position."[47] Accepting exploitive terms due to one's inferior social position is the opposite of accepting terms as a free and equal citizen. It should be added that 'arbitrary contingencies' also fail to satisfy the reasonableness requirement. That one occupies a particular social position or has a superior endowment of talents are largely matters of social and genetic contingency; they are not considerations that one can reasonably use to justify one's preferred terms of cooperation.[48] In light of the above, it seems plausible enough to think that reasonableness requires placing knowledge of talents and social positions behind the veil of ignorance. Though an agreement informed by such knowledge could very well be a rational one, it might not also be a reasonable one.

It should be noted that the Rawlsian manner of specifying the content of procedural fairness has conceptual significance. If reciprocity were enough to supply the content of procedural fairness, then Rawls's understanding of justice's narrowness would be preserved. Like procedural fairness, reciprocity is not a value that must be traded off against other values when determining which regulatory principles populate the reasonable set of alternatives. Regulatory principles that would be selected via the original position are mutually acceptable, as well as mutually beneficial, and thus fully meet the reciprocity criterion. This is not to say that reciprocity does not admit of degrees; societies undoubtedly realize its requirements to greater and lesser extents. From the perspective of reciprocity, however, shortfalls in a society's level of fairness track the extent to which it falls short of its institutional regulatory principles, rather than the extent to which it fall short of a more fundamental, substantive principle of distributive fairness. If the content of procedural fairness can be specified without relying on a distributive ideal, then our institutional regulatory principles could be understood as principles that fully express the normative requirements of fairness. We would be able to retain the thought that they are principles that specify the content of justice, that is, principles that tell us what justice is, and that they should therefore not be understood as principles that represents a compromise between justice and other values, that is, principles that tell us what is morally required of us, all things, including justice, considered.

There is a problem, however. Though the regulatory principles we adopt must certainly meet a criterion of reasonableness, the idea of reasonableness is not itself sufficient to explain why knowledge of talents and social positions must be placed behind the veil of ignorance. Reasonableness imposes a constraint on the kinds of reasons hypothetical contractors may give to each other in the original position. Contractors might point to the fact that a set of principles will safeguard all of their basic needs or that it meets the requirements of publicity. What they cannot do is attempt to coerce or pressure each other into an agreement that some find less acceptable than others or offer each other morally arbitrary considerations. Considering that this is what reasonableness requires, it is consistent for hypothetical contractors to retain knowledge of their social positions and talents, yet bargain in accordance with the requirements of reasonableness. Reasonableness is thus indeterminate between a description of the original positon where knowledge of social positions and talents are behind the original positon, and a description where they have this knowledge but bargain in a reasonable manner.

One factor that might be thought to favor withholding knowledge of talents and social positions is the importance of determinacy. As Rawls notes in *A Theory of Justice*, one of the functions of withholding knowledge of particulars is to remove the various factors that lead to disagreement between citizens, thereby ensuring that a certain, determinate set of principles would be agreed upon.[49] Such particulars include knowledge of one's talents, class, conception of the good, special psychological features, and the economic and political situation of one's society.[50] Determinacy is not sufficient to justify withholding knowledge of all particulars, however. Knowledge of at least some of these particulars could presumably be let through without jeopardizing it. What's more, knowledge of certain particulars would presumably affect the content of what is agreed to. For example, imagine that hypothetical contractors have knowledge of their talents and are seeking to agree upon terms of cooperation in a reasonable manner. Those with greater talents cannot propose that they be given a superior share of primary goods simply on the ground that they possess greater talent. The fact that they have greater talent is morally arbitrary and is thus not a reasonable consideration to offer. What they could propose, however, is that they be permitted a *relatively* greater share of goods in the event that they choose to exercise their talents in ways that will afford the less talented a greater *absolute* amount of goods. Such a proposal is one that would be both reasonable and rational for the less talented to accept. Reasonableness does not, however, require that the more talented propose terms of cooperation that *maximally* benefit the less talented. The promise of benefit is necessary, but promising maximal benefit is to go quite a bit further than that.[51] Maximal benefit only follows when knowledge of talents is placed behind the veil of ignorance. Without knowledge of whether one is talented or untalented, it makes sense to opt specifically for maximal benefit to the worst-off, given a certain set of assumptions, such as that a unit of primary goods carries more value when a person has fewer of them.[52] With knowledge of talents in hand, however, it would be irrational for the talented to choose maximal benefit over mere benefit, and reasonableness is consistent with either kind of benefit

(c) The Role of Substantive Fairness in Specifying a Fair Contract Situation

In the previous section, I argued that the idea of reasonableness, and thus of reciprocity, is not sufficient to justify a particular description of our hypothetical contract situation. Though any considerations we offer in favor of a particular description must themselves be reasonable ones drawn from our shared political culture, the idea of reasonableness is not enough on its own. In particular, reasonableness is indeterminate between (a) concealing all knowledge of particulars behind the veil of ignorance and (b) permitting some knowledge (such as knowledge of talents) on the condition that deliberators make use of it in a reasonable manner. As a result, the ideas of reasonableness and reciprocity cannot, at least on their own, solve the problem of arbitrariness and secure the legitimacy of our institutional regulatory principles.

In this section, I argue that we should we draw upon a different idea of fairness to secure legitimacy. The idea of fairness I think we should draw upon to justify (a number of) the details of the original position is the idea specified by luck egalitarianism. Luck egalitarianism can straightforwardly justify concealing knowledge of social position and natural talents. Though reasonableness is indeterminate between placing such knowledge behind the veil of ignorance and constraining the manner in which that knowledge is used, luck equality is not. One's talents and social position are largely traceable to brute luck, after all. They belong as much to one's circumstances as they do to one's choices. Even when the arguments that better-situated contractors make are reasonable, using knowledge of one's better circumstances to secure a greater relative share is unfair from a luck egalitarian perspective. Luck egalitarianism can thus account for why securing a fair contract situation requires withholding knowledge of these particulars.

It might seem implausible at first to think that luck egalitarianism is embedded in our shared political culture, since there are many political philosophers who have found luck egalitarianism implausible. However, I think the plausibility of identifying luck egalitarian fairness as part of our shared political culture increases dramatically when it is understood to be a conception of a fundamental value. As I argued in Chapter 3, many of the objections that theorists have offered to luck egalitarianism are only damaging to the theory when it is understood as a theory of all-things-considered institutional rightness. Anderson's concerns about harshness, Scheffler's worries about an implausible conception of freewill, and Wolff's concerns about a conflict between luck equality and respect, though collectively quite powerful against a regulatory version of luck egalitarianism, instead just constrain its implementation when luck egalitarianism is understood as a conception of a fundamental value. Furthermore, I have argued that luck egalitarianism does an admirable job of achieving coherence with a core range of central, widely shared intuitive judgments. On the one hand, it contains the idea that it is unfair for someone to be less well-off through no fault of her own. As a result, it accounts for the judgment that it is unfair for the social group or economic class into which one is born to negatively affect one's life prospects, as well as for the judgment that it is unfair for disabilities attributable to misfortune to do so. What's more, luck egalitarianism also contains the idea that it is unfair to subsidize people for their choices, thereby accounting for the judgment that it is fair for the unlucky gambler or the leisure-loving surfer to have less than others. Considering that all of these are widely shared judgments embedded in our political culture, I do not think it is unreasonable to conclude that the value they express is embedded in our political culture. Furthermore, since luck egalitarianism, in its most plausible form, is specifically an account of that value's content, I do not think it is unreasonable to conclude that if luck equality accurately captures that value (as I have argued it does), then it too is a part of our political culture.

Interestingly (though not surprisingly), the principle of luck equality also plays a role in specifying the details of Ronald Dworkin's chosen procedural device. Recall that though Dworkin deems the ideal of an ambition-sensitive but endowment-insensitive distribution to be unsuitable for purposes of guiding political practice, he nonetheless models his hypothetical insurance device after it. His thought is that hypothetical insurance provides a fair way to place limitations on compensation, as there is a sense in which hypothetical insurance converts cases of incompensable bad brute luck into cases of bad option luck. After all, cases of bad brute luck are only incompensable if and insofar as one would, hypothetically, have *chosen* not to insure against them.[53] Though hypothetical insurance supplies a form of procedural fairness that appeals to luck equality, there are difficulties with it that nonetheless make a suitably described version of the original position a better option, in my opinion. As we noted in Chapter 3, Dworkin is vulnerable to the harshness objection, as it is not clear that hypothetical insurance can justify securing basic needs against bad option luck across the board. Though it is likely rational for hypothetical insurance buyers to insure against the possibility that future imprudence might, at some point, endanger the satisfaction of their basic needs, Kok-Chor Tan is probably right to claim that an insurance policy that protects basic needs without any stipulations about disqualifying forms of imprudence would have prohibitively high premiums.[54] The problem with the insurance device, then, is not that it fails to satisfy the requirements of luck equality. The problem is that its output does not give enough weight to compassion, and that it thereby fails to choose from within the range of plausible outputs. Just as the choice between outputs is specifically a choice between plausible outputs, so too is the choice between procedural devices specially a choice between those that select from the set of plausible outputs.

If luck egalitarianism supplies the fairness criterion we use to non-arbitrarily specify the details of our hypothetical contract situation, then it enters a theory of institutional rightness in two places: first, as one of the competing fundamental values that must be weighed against each other when formulating the regulatory principles that constitute the set of plausible options, and second, as a criterion in light of which we non-arbitrarily specify the details of our procedural device. It might seem peculiar that the same value should enter our theory in these two different places. One worry is that using luck equality in both the procedural and trade-off levels makes us vulnerable to what some have called the 'rigging objection,' that is, the objection that it is circular to specify the details of our procedural device in such a way that it yields the regulatory outcome we wanted to achieve in any case. This objection has sometimes been pushed against Rawls in light of the fact that he also justifies his principles via the method of reflective equilibrium and thus that his contract device seems designed to yield principles he antecedently decided had the best fit with our all-things-considered judgments.[55] However, I think that the rigging objection is unfounded when applied to my use of luck egalitarianism. Specifying the details of the original position in light of a luck egalitarian standard is not the same thing as, say, deciding upon a more equality-heavy trade-off package in advance and then rigging the details of the original position to ensure that it picks out that package. If rigging the procedure in order to get a more equality-heavy outcome is what we cared about, then there are lots of ways we could go about doing that. We might, for example, describe the parties to the contract as being so risk averse that they would be inclined towards equality even when they possess knowledge of their talents and social position. We might also characterize the parties as envious beings who strongly dislike the prospect of other people potentially having more than them. The reasons we do not make these adjustments is because using luck egalitarianism to choose between different descriptions of the original position is not the same thing as rigging our description to produce a more egalitarian output. The principle of luck equality, when applied to an assessment of the details of the original position, recommends that knowledge of social position and natural talents be withheld. Since one's social position and talents are largely products of brute luck, and since having knowledge of them would give some parties a bargaining advantage over others, luck egalitarianism requires that they be placed behind the veil of ignorance for the sake of ensuring a fair contract situation. In contrast, nothing about luck egalitarianism suggests that the fairness of the contract situation requires parties to be motivated by risk aversion or envy. Though risk aversion and envy would have the effect of producing a more egalitarian regulatory output, such motivations do not make the original position a fairer contract situation. I thus do not think the rigging objection should prevent us from employing luck egalitarian fairness as both a value present in the trade-off packages we are adjudicating between and as a criterion in light of which to justify our description of the original position. To the contrary, using luck egalitarianism at the procedural level helps to answer the rigging objection, as it provides us with a resource in light of which to choose between possible descriptions of the original position without relying on antecedent moral judgments about which of the plausible regulatory options is best.

It should be noted that I do not mean to argue for a luck egalitarian interpretation of Rawls. Whether Rawls should be understood as a sort of incipient or proto-luck egalitarian is a sticky issue that I do not wish to take a stance on here.[56] I think luck egalitarianism can be used to specify a particular description of the original position, but this is compatible with both luck egalitarian and non-luck egalitarian interpretations of Rawls's work. On the one hand, if it turns out that Rawls is implicitly committed to a form of luck egalitarianism, then luck equality is a resource internal to his theory that can be drawn upon to justify a particular description of the original position. On the other hand, if it turns out that Rawls is not implicitly committed to luck egalitarianism, then luck equality is a resource external to his theory that might nonetheless be used to improve upon or supplement it. Whether luck equality is best understood as an internal resource or an external supplement is not a question I need to answer for purposes of the present argument.

An account of procedural fairness is an important part of solving the arbitrariness problem, and thus it is also an important part of justifying the coercive imposition of institutional regulatory principles. It should be noted, however, that there are some situations where we can make justified decisions about regulatory principles without using a procedure. Procedural fairness is specifically useful for non-arbitrarily deciding the right trade-off points between conflicting values. It is therefore not needed in cases where we can increase the extent to which one or more values are realized without also decreasing the extent to which other values are realized. Such a case was discussed near the end of Chapter 3. There, I argued that the regulatory appeal of the difference principle is importantly contingent. Among other things, I argued that once the implementation of Rawls's liberty and fair equality of opportunity principles has achieved a society where inequality between racial and social groups has largely been eliminated, the scrutiny needed in order to distribute benefits conditionally would no longer fall disproportionately on particular groups, and thus the tension between luck equality and respect that Jonathan Wolff highlights would be alleviated. I recommended that in such circumstances, a version of the difference principle that maximizes the position of those with bad brute luck but only provides a sufficientarian floor for the imprudent would realize a greater amount of fundamental justice without loss to either respect or compassion and would thus be preferable, all things considered. Since the recommended modification would achieve an increase in fundamental justice without a corresponding decrease in values that normally conflict with it, procedural fairness has no role to play.

To summarize my argument thus far, I have claimed that a disagreement over the way fairness should be understood is what divides contextualists and pluralists. Pluralists, on the one hand, think of fairness as a substantive fundamental value, one that is necessary but not sufficient for the justification of institutional regulatory principles. Though they think fairness must have some say over the content of optimal regulatory principles, they also think it must leave room for the requirements of other important values. It follows from this view that there is an important distinction to be made between a conception of what justice is and a conception of what is institutionally required of us, all things, including justice, considered. Since optimal institutional regulatory principles are imperfectly fair by their very nature, they are also imperfectly just (in the narrow sense of the word) and are thus not identical with justice itself. To give an account of the content of justice itself is to give an account of the fairness input that regulatory principles only partially reflect, an account that must either implicitly or explicitly draw a line between considerations internal and external to that input.

Contextualists like Rawls, in contrast, understand fairness to be procedural. Though Rawls also thinks fairness is central to the justification of institutional regulatory principles, he does not think of it as one of the competing values expressed in value trade-off packages. Since there is more than one plausible weighting of the different values that institutional regulatory principles reflect, some method via which to non-arbitrarily choose between packages is needed. Without such a method, we would not be able to say that the package we select reflects citizens' collective political obligations and thus would not be able to legitimately impose its requirements in a coercive manner. In light of this, Rawls understands fairness not as a property that regulatory principles possess to a greater or lesser degree, depending on the extent to which they conform to a fundamental principle of distributive fairness, but as a property that regulatory principles either do or do not possess, depending on whether they would be hypothetically selected in an optimally fair contract situation. When fairness is understood this way, it is no longer inappropriate to think of a conception of institutional regulation as a conception of what justice is. Since the source of regulatory fairness lies in the procedure via which regulatory principles are selected, rather than in a substantive principle of pure distributive fairness that they only partially conform to, the distinction between what justice is and what is institutionally required of us, all things, including justice, considered, seemingly breaks down. There is no longer a more fundamental principle of distributive fairness that institutional regulatory principles fall short of and thus no longer a sense in which to say that they are non-identical with distributive justice itself.

If my analysis of the problem of arbitrariness is correct, however, then the above-described Rawlsian rejection of the distinction between justice itself and all-things-considered institutional rightness is ill-advised. Though a procedural understanding of fairness is indeed needed in order to solve the problem of arbitrariness and thus to confer legitimacy upon our institutional regulatory principles, it cannot do the job by itself. A thorough solution to the problem requires a non-arbitrary way to specify the details of the hypothetical contract situation, and pluralist justice, specifically defeasible luck equality, gives us precisely that. It provides us with a criterion in light of which to judge the fairness of the contract situation itself, and thus with a basis upon which to address the problem of arbitrariness at the procedural level. The conceptual situation changes when substantive fairness is used in this way. If Rawls's principles are allegedly fair because they were chosen in the original position, and the original position is fair only in light of a more ultimate principle of distributive fairness, then the output of the original position, if found wanting in light of that more ultimate principle, cannot be completely fair. In other words, to think that the original position confers unqualified fairness upon its output involves a failure to evaluate that output in light of the more fundamental criterion of fairness that the original position itself relies upon. If I am right, then the pluralist distinction between a conception of what justice is and a conception of what is institutionally required of us, all things, including justice, considered, holds. The output of the original position cannot be identical with distributive justice because it relies upon and only partially conforms to a more fundamental principle of distributive fairness.

A further upshot of my solution to the problem of arbitrariness is that it reconciles two seemingly conflicting ideas: (a) the idea that narrow justice is one value among many, and (b) the idea that narrow justice is the first virtue of institutions. As we noted in our discussion of the view that fairness is but one of the substantive values internal to justice, attempting to merge (a) and (b) by turning narrow justice into a complex value lands us in a morass of conceptual confusion. Though understanding narrow justice as a complex value gives it the weight it seemingly needs in order to qualify as the first virtue of institutions, it makes no sense to think of luck egalitarian fairness as one of the simple values comprising narrow justice. If fairness is a simple value, then narrow justice just is that value, and whatever weighty, all-things-considered principles we think are best for the institutional context will be principles expressing what broad justice (or rightness) requires in that context. However, if my understanding of the theoretical role of luck egalitarian fairness is correct, then understanding narrow justice as a simple value need not prevent us from also understanding it as the first virtue of institutions. On my understanding, justice is unique among the values institutional regulatory principles reflect because it enters a theory of regulatory justice at the both the procedural and value trade-off levels. Unlike the other values that must be traded off against each other (e.g., efficiency, compassion, etc.), justice plays a key role in determining the shape of the hypothetical contract situation. As such, it also plays a key role in solving the arbitrariness problem and thus in ensuring the legitimacy of coercively enforcing the institutional regulatory principles selected. There is thus a very real sense in which justice is of primary significance in the institutional context. Unless our all-things-considered institutional principles are hypothetically selected in an optimally fair contract situation, the coercive legitimacy of the institutions deigned in light of them is jeopardized. But unless the contract situation satisfies the requirements of luck egalitarian justice, then the fairness of that situation is itself jeopardized. Justice is thus a particularly key value with respect to the justification of institutional regulatory principles. Not only does their moral desirability depend upon whether they give adequate weight to it, but their coercive legitimacy depends upon whether the procedure that hypothetically selects them meets its requirements.

5. Conclusion

In conclusion, the purpose of this chapter was to establish the plausibility of understanding justice as one fundamental value among many. First, I explained that pluralists think justice is distinct from all-things-considered principles because the all-things-considered optimality of those principles requires deviating somewhat from distributive fairness. Second, I argued that the dispute between pluralists and contextualists over justice's narrowness is more than verbal because it reflects an underlying theoretical disagreement over the way fairness should be interpreted. Finally, I argued that the rationale for rejecting a substantive interpretation of fairness in favor of a procedural interpretation, when consistently applied to the selection of procedural devices, requires us to employ substantive fairness at the procedural level. Without a substantive principle of distributive fairness, we cannot justify the claim that our procedural device is itself fair and thus cannot resolve the problem that arbitrariness poses for the justified exercise of state coercion. If my analysis is correct, then justice is both a defeasible value *and* the first virtue of specifically *coercive* institutions.

Notes

1. See Cohen (2008) Chapter 7.
2. See section 3(b) in Chapter 3 of this book.
3. Cohen (2008) pp. 156–61.
4. See Segall (2007) pp. 188–91; Swift (2008) pp. 382–7; Tomlin (2010) p. 244; Quong (2010) pp. 315–6 and pp. 336–40; and Gilabert (2012) pp. 112–4.
5. For the term 'complex value,' see Quong (2010) p. 337.
6. Quong (2010) pp. 337–40.
7. See Gilabert (2012) p. 107 for the term 'non-trumping value.' See pages 106–8 for his general discussion of justice's plural grounds.
8. See Quong's comments in Quong (2010) pp. 321–6.
9. Segall (2007) p. 188; Swift (2008) p. 382–3; Tomlin (2010) p. 244.
10. It is perhaps a testament to the appeal of the above-described view that Cohen was to some extent tempted by it. Though Cohen sometimes seems to think that nothing but distributive fairness is internal to justice, in *Why Not Socialism?* he expresses some uncertainty about whether community is internal (Cohen 2009 p. 37), and in "Fairness and Legitimacy in Justice" he concedes that justice also has a historical component that he, as the title suggests, calls 'legitimacy' (Cohen 2011). Though I agree that justice and legitimacy have an important relationship with each other, one that I explore in both this chapter and the next, I also think it is a mistake to claim that fairness is but one of the values internal to justice, a mistake I explain in the present section.
11. Aristotle (1998) Book V, Sections 1–2. See also Waldron (2003) p. 274.
12. Rawls (1971) p. 3.
13. See Rawls's and Cohen's discussions of the term 'intuitionism' in Rawls (1971) p. 35; and Cohen (2008) p. 4.
14. See Rawls (1971) pp. 12–3 and pp. 118–20.
15. See Rawls's comments in Rawls (1971) pp. 12–3.
16. For discussions of the extent to which Rawls and Cohen are and are not compatible, see Williams (2008) pp. 117–26; Tomlin (2012); and Valentini (2012) pp. 657–8.
17. As far as I know, my understanding of the difference between virtue ethics and the other major moral theories is the standard one. See, for instance, Hursthouse (2013), especially the discussion of the application problem in section 3.
18. Rawls (1971) pp. 12–3.
19. See Dworkin (2000) pp. 1–4; and Kymlicka (2002) pp. 1–5.
20. See Tomlin (2010) pp. 233–4.
21. Kymlicka (2002) pp. 3–4.
22. Dworkin (2000) p. 1.
23. Kymlicka (2002) pp. 32–3.
24. Dworkin (2002) pp. 120–1; and Dworkin (2003) pp. 190–1.
25. Dworkin (2002) pp. 122–4.
26. The concept of citizens' good is expressed consistently across the interpretations of abstract equality Kymlicka explores in *Contemporary Political Philosophy*.

Sometimes other words are used (e.g., preferences, ends, etc.), but the concept is still there. See, for example, Kymlicka (2002) pp. 32–3, pp. 64–5, pp. 75–8, and pp. 107–10.

27. My thoughts about the difference between 'efficiency' and 'concern' to some extent mirror Kymlicka's thoughts about the difference between egalitarian and teleological versions of utilitarianism. See Kymlicka (2002) pp. 32–7.
28. For Cohen's discussion of the claim that justice is the first virtue of institutions, see Cohen (2008) pp. 302–6.
29. See Rawls's and Cohen's discussions of 'intuitionism' in Rawls (1971) p. 35; and Cohen (2008) p. 4.
30. Rawls (1971) pp. 36–7.
31. Rawls (1971) p. 36 and p. 41.
32. For a related discussion of the relationship between contractualism and interpersonal justification, see Anderson (2010).
33. See Rawls (1971) pp. 42–4.
34. Rawls's justification for the priority of liberty over other primary goods can be found in Rawls (1971) pp. 541–8. A more comprehensive discussion of the matter can be found in Rawls (1993) pp. 289–371.
35. For the contrast between goods and functions, see Stocker (1997) pp. 202–3.
36. Rawls (1971) pp. 17–22.
37. For other discussions of the original position, see Dworkin (1989); and Nagel (1989).
38. Rawls (1993) p. 25 for the first quote and p. 22 for the second quote.
39. Rawls (1971) p. 115.
40. Rawls (1993) pp. 18–9. For a more elaborate description of his political conception of the person, see Rawls (1993) pp. 29–35.
41. For work critical of the claim that the self can be stripped of its properties, especially its conception of the good, see Sandel (1982) and Sandel (1984).
42. For a discussion of the role our shared political culture plays in justifying institutional principles, see Rawls (1985) pp. 228–31. See also Rawls (1993) pp. 8–11 and pp. 12–5.
43. Rawls (1993) pp. 52–3.
44. Rawls (1993) p. 17.
45. Rawls (1993) p. 16.
46. Rawls (1993) pp. 48–54.
47. Rawls (1999) pp. 136–7.
48. See Rawls (1985) p. 237; and Rawls (1993) pp. 24–5.
49. Rawls (1971) pp. 139–40.
50. Rawls (1971) p. 137.
51. For the distinction between inequalities that benefit the worst-off and those that *maximally* benefit the worst-off, see Rawls (1971) pp. 78–9.
52. See Rawls (1971) pp. 154–5 and 542–3.
53. Dworkin (2000) pp. 73–7.
54. Tan (2008) pp. 678–9.
55. For an excellent discussion of the rigging objection, see Daniels (1996) Chapter 3.
56. For work that suggests Rawls, though not a full-blown luck egalitarian, is nonetheless motivated by luck egalitarian concerns, see Kymlicka (2002) pp. 57–75; and Cohen (2008) pp. 152–61. For arguments against interpreting Rawls as a quasi-luck egalitarian, see Scheffler (2003) pp. 24–31; and Anderson (2010) pp. 6–12.

References

Anderson, Elizabeth. 2010. "The Fundamental Disagreement between Luck Egalitarians and Relational Egalitarians." *Canadian Journal of Philosophy* 40(suppl. 1): 1–23.

Aristotle. 1998. *Aristotle: The Nicomachean Ethics*. Trans. W.D. Ross (Oxford: Oxford University Press).
Berlin, Isaiah. 2002. "Two Concepts of Liberty." In *Liberty: Incorporating Four Essays on Liberty*. Ed. Henry Hardy (Oxford: Oxford University Press).
Cohen, G.A. 2008. *Rescuing Justice and Equality* (Cambridge, MA: Harvard University Press).
Cohen, G.A. 2009. *Why Not Socialism?* (Princeton: Princeton University Press).
Cohen, G.A. 2011. "Fairness and Legitimacy in Justice, and: Does Option Luck Ever Preserve Justice?" In *On the Currency of Egalitarian Justice, and Other Essays in Political Philosophy*. Ed. Michael Otsuka (Princeton: Princeton University Press). Pp. 124–43.
Daniels, Norman. 1996. *Justice and Justification: Reflective Equilibrium in Theory and Practice* (Cambridge: Cambridge University Press).
Dworkin, Ronald. 1989. "The Original Position." In *Reading Rawls: Critical Studies on Rawls' 'A Theory of Justice'*. Ed. Normal Daniels (Stanford: Stanford University Press). Pp. 16–53.
Dworkin, Ronald. 2000. *Sovereign Virtue: The Theory and Practice of Equality* (Cambridge, MA: Harvard University Press).
Dworkin, Ronald. 2002. "*Sovereign Virtue* Revisited." *Ethics* 113: 106–43.
Dworkin, Ronald. 2003. "Equality, Luck and Hierarchy." *Philosophy and Public Affairs* 31: 190–8.
Feinberg, Joel. 1989. "Rawls and Intuitionism." In *Reading Rawls: Critical Studies on Rawls' 'A Theory of Justice'*. Ed. Normal Daniels (Stanford: Stanford University Press). Pp. 108–24.
Gilabert, Pablo. 2012. "Cohen on Socialism, Equality and Community." *Socialist Studies* 8: 101–21.
Hursthouse, Rosalind. 2013. "Virtue Ethics." In *The Stanford Encyclopedia of Philosophy*. Ed. Edward N. Zalta. Available at http://plato.stanford.edu/archives/fall2013/entries/ethics-virtue/
Kymlicka, Will. 2002. *Contemporary Political Philosophy: An Introduction* (New York: Oxford University Press).
Miller, David. 2007. *National Responsibility and Global Justice* (Oxford: Oxford University Press).
Nagel, Thomas. 1989. "Rawls on Justice." In *Reading Rawls: Critical Studies on Rawls' 'A Theory of Justice'*. Ed. Normal Daniels (Stanford: Stanford University Press). Pp. 1–16.
Nozick, Robert. 1974. *Anarchy, State, and Utopia* (New York: Basic Books).
Quong, Jonathan. 2010. "Justice Beyond Equality." *Social Theory and Practice* 36: 315–40.
Rawls, John. 1971. *A Theory of Justice* (Cambridge, MA: Belknap Press).
Rawls, John. 1985. "Justice as Fairness: Political Not Metaphysical." *Philosophy and Public Affairs* 14: 223–51.
Rawls, John. 1993. *Political Liberalism* (New York: Columbia University Press).
Rawls, John. 1999. *The Law of Peoples with "The Idea of Public Reason Revisited."* (Cambridge, MA: Harvard University Press).
Rawls, John. 2001. *Justice as Fairness: A Restatement*. Ed. Erin Kelly (Cambridge, MA: Belknap Press).
Sandel, Michael. 1982. *Liberalism and the Limits of Justice* (Cambridge: Cambridge University Press).

Sandel, Michael. 1984. "The Procedural Republic and the Unencumbered Self." *Political Theory* 12: 81–96.

Scheffler, Samuel. 2003. "What Is Egalitarianism?" *Philosophy and Public Affairs* 31: 5–39.

Segall, Shlomi. 2007. "In Solidarity with the Imprudent: A Defense of Luck Egalitarianism." *Social Theory and Practice* 33: 177–98.

Stocker, Michael. 1997. "Abstract and Concrete Value: Plurality, Conflict, and Maximization." In *Incommensurability, Incomparability, and Practical Reason*. Ed. Ruth Chang (Cambridge, MA: Harvard University Press).

Swift, Adam. 2008. "The Value of Philosophy in Non-Ideal Circumstances." *Social Theory and Practice* 34: 363–87.

Tan, Kok-Chor. 2004. *Justice without Borders* (Cambridge: Cambridge University Press).

Tan, Kok-Chor. 2008. "A Defense of Luck Egalitarianism." *The Journal of Philosophy* 105: 665–90.

Tomlin, Patrick. 2010. "Survey Article: Internal Doubts about Cohen's Rescue of Justice." *The Journal of Political Philosophy* 18: 228–47.

Tomlin, Patrick. 2012. "Can I be a Luck Egalitarian and a Rawlsian?" *Ethical Perspectives* 19: 371–97.

Valentini, Laura. 2012. "Ideal vs. Non-ideal Theory: A Conceptual Map." *Philosophy Compass* 7: 654–64.

Waldron, Jeremy. 2003. "The Primacy of Justice." *Legal Theory* 9: 269–94.

Williams, Andrew. 2008. "Justice, Incentives and Constructivism." *Ratio* 21 (2008): 476–93. Reprinted in *Justice, Equality, and Constructivism: Essays on G.A. Cohen's Rescuing Justice and Equality*. Ed. Brian Feltham (Chichester: Wiley-Blackwell, 2009). Pp. 110–26.

6 Fairness and Democratic Legitimacy

1. Introduction

Completely eliminating arbitrariness from our institutional principles requires more than a principled way of specifying the content of procedural fairness. To completely eliminate arbitrariness, we must establish beyond any reasonable disagreement that (a) the institutional principles adopted are fair to citizens and (b) the institutional arrangements via which we have decided to implement those principles are better than alternative implementation strategies. But is it possible to completely avoid reasonable disagreement about these matters?

In section 2, I use the philosophical literature about democracy to address the threat that reasonable disagreement about the above questions poses for legitimacy. As a survey of the literature reveals, contemporary political philosophers tend to understand democracy as a legitimate way of handling reasonable disagreement about which laws to enact.[1] If contemporary theorists are right about this, then democracy can handle reasonable disagreement that stems from differences of opinion over which institutional principles are fair, as well as disagreement that stems from differences of opinion over how best to implement a set of principles.

In addition to drawing upon democratic theory, I also contribute to it by arguing (in section 3) that my previous chapter's conclusion concerning the relationship between substantive and procedural fairness can be usefully applied here. In my view, contemporary theorists struggle to offer a theory of democracy that both avoids reasonable objection and is sufficient to explain democratic legitimacy. Against this background, I argue that substantive fairness (i.e., pluralist justice) supplies a surprisingly promising solution to the problem that reasonable disagreement poses for democracy. Although we can reasonably disagree about some of the requirements of substantive fairness, there is nonetheless widespread agreement that fairness require an equal distribution of liberties, the right to vote included. In this way, democratic procedures are a basic, uncontroversial requirement of substantive fairness.

In section 4, I respond to two objections, the first of which notes that democratic procedures are not sufficient to secure legitimacy, as highly immoral laws are illegitimate even if democratically enacted, and the second of which argues that I mistakenly treat legitimacy as if it is a binary concept.

2. Democracy and Reasonable Disagreement

Coercion, by definition, infringes upon liberty. And assuming that liberty is an especially valuable good, coercing someone is a prima facie wrong. In light of its problematic status, liberals maintain that coercion is only legitimate when it can be justified to those whose liberty is infringed upon.

If it were the case that everyone agreed upon moral and political matters, justification would not be difficult. Assuming the state's decisions were in conformity with commonly held principles, one could simply refer to those principles to justify the state's laws. Unfortunately, most liberal democracies are characterized by widespread disagreement about moral and political matters. As a result, one cannot assume in advance that citizens will accept any justificatory principles that might be invoked. Nor, for that matter, can it be assumed that citizens *should* accept those principles, as citizens may have reasonable objections that their own, equally reasonable principles are not vulnerable to.[2]

In the previous chapter, we considered one important way in which reasonable agreement threatens legitimacy. We noted that citizens may reasonably disagree over the weights we should assign to competing political values, and on that basis, that they may reasonably disagree over which institutional regulatory principles are most justified. We also noted that contractualist procedural fairness supplies a potential solution to this problem. If citizens situated in an optimally fair bargaining situation would hypothetically agree to a particular set of regulatory principles, then we have a justification available for why those principles are the ones we appeal to when designing our shared, coercive institutions. We can tell the naysayers that these are the principles that they themselves would choose if freed from the personal biases and other contingencies that normally prevent consensus. But does this contractualist justification actually suffice to secure legitimacy? Perhaps not. There are a number of areas where reasonable disagreement about institutional regulatory principles is possible. One area we have already discussed is the content of contractualist procedural fairness. I argued that substantive fairness can be usefully applied to determine the content of a fair hypothetical contract situation, and on that basis, that there is a special connection between substantive fairness and legitimacy.

Though I think using substantive fairness to justify a particular description of our hypothetical contract situation is useful for addressing the problem that reasonable disagreement poses for our institutional regulatory principles, difficulties remain. Even if we can specify a uniquely fair contract situation, it remains possible for there to be reasonable disagreement over what principles would be chosen in that situation. What if we were to expand the list of regulatory principles from which to choose? Rawls is primarily concerned with choosing between the principle of average utility and the difference principle.

In the previous chapter, I considered a choice between two different versions of the difference principle: a version that requires *maximum* benefit for the least well-off and a version that merely requires *some* benefit. But these possibilities are not exhaustive. For example, how might the principle of average utility fare if it were supplemented with a sufficientarian floor? Ensuring that all citizens' basic needs would be met removes much of the risk associated with choosing the principle of average utility, and opting for utility maximization instead of the difference principle promises greater gains for those who turn out to have economically productive talents. This and other possibilities would have to be considered if we are to avoid the charge that our list of alternatives is arbitrary, and the longer the list of alternatives is, the more likely it is that there will be reasonable disagreement over what would be hypothetically selected.

Consider also the possibility of reasonable disagreement over how to implement our institutional regulatory principles. What institutional arrangements would successfully implement a principle like the difference principle? Rawls argues that what he calls a "property owning democracy" would successfully institutionalize his principles,[3] but it is worth noting that there are other reasonable possibilities. In fact, Rawls notes that a "liberal socialist regime" with public ownership of the means of production seems equally promising.[4] That there can be reasonable disagreement over how to institutionalize a set of principles is also exemplified in a dispute between G. A. Cohen and Richard Arneson over the merits of socialism. Whereas Cohen maintains that socialism is a superior means of institutionalizing the requirements of community and luck egalitarian fairness, Arneson argues for capitalism.[5]

The pervasiveness of reasonable disagreement is well-appreciated by theorists who work on democratic theory. In fact, the importance of democracy is typically understood against the background of reasonable disagreement. The general thought is that even if citizens disagree with a particular law, the fact that it was democratically enacted provides a justification for why they should accept that law as binding. This justification, theorists maintain, is one that citizens can reasonably accept (or at least cannot reasonably reject), even if they still have reason to prefer that the law never have been passed and/or that it be repealed in future legislation. What theorists tend to disagree about, however, is the content of democratic justification. According to one strand of thought, democratic procedures are a form of imperfect procedural justice; they tend to produce independently "correct" outputs. On this view, the justificatory value of democracy lies in its instrumental significance.[6] According to another strand, however, democratic procedures are more akin to pure procedural justice; democratic outputs are fair to citizens because they were enacted via an intrinsically fair set of procedures.[7]

If democratic theorists are right about the function of democracy, then democracy supplies a convenient solution to the above-described difficulties. Though we may not be able to completely eliminate reasonable disagreement surrounding our institutional regulatory principles, we also do not have to. Whatever reasonable disagreement there may be over enacted laws is addressable so long as those laws were enacted democratically. This includes disagreement that stems from disagreement over our regulatory principles. If someone objects to a law because they reasonably disagree with the principles it institutionalizes, then the fact that the law was democratically enacted can be invoked to justify it to her. Similarly, a law's democratic credentials may be used to justify it to someone who thinks an alternative law would institutionalize those principles better.

Convenient though democracy is, the fact that we must resort to it casts serious doubt on the contextualist understanding of primacy. On the contextualist understanding, the fact that we appeal to institutional regulatory principles to guide political practice makes it appropriate to think of them as the 'first virtue of institutions.' However, as the worries we have described suggest, appealing to a principle like the difference principle does not suffice to secure a law's legitimacy. Such an appeal may not even be necessary, as presumably one need not appeal specifically to the difference principle if there are other reasonable principles one might appeal to when justifying a proposed law before a legislative assembly. It is thus false that institutions must conform to a particular set of regulatory principles in order to be acceptable. Though presumably laws must be given a reasonable justification before being voted upon, no particular set of principles is either necessary or sufficient for securing legitimacy. What does the legitimizing, thereby rendering a law acceptable, is the fact that it was enacted democratically. But why do democratic procedures have this legitimizing power? What is it about democracy that makes it a fair way of addressing reasonable disagreement?

In order for an understanding of the content of democratic justification to be plausible, it is necessary that the justification given in support of that understanding be free of reasonable disagreement. After all, if democratic procedures function to secure legitimacy by providing citizens with an acceptable justification for objectionable laws, it would be a serious problem if that justification itself depended on principles that are vulnerable to reasonable objection. Such a justification would simply move the problem of reasonable disagreement up to a different level, from disagreement over laws to disagreement over what would constitute an acceptable justification for those laws. In the next section, I will argue that leading theories of democracy have difficulty providing an explanation for democratic legitimacy that both avoids reasonable disagreement and is sufficient to explain democracy's importance. The alternative that I will recommend is that we turn to substantive fairness in order to explain the fairness of democratic procedures. If the arguments I provide are successful, then my earlier claim that substantive fairness has a special relationship with legitimacy is further supported, and, therefore, so too is my claim that substantive fairness is the first virtue of institutions.

3. Theorizing Democracy

As I mentioned, one strand of thought within democratic theory maintains that democracy secures legitimacy via an instrumental justification. It holds that democratic outputs are justifiable to citizens on the grounds that democracy is a heuristic device used to improve our political track record. In some versions of this view, democracy's instrumental significance is cashed out specifically with reference to the quality of that which is legislated. In other versions, democracy's instrumental significance is understood more broadly, as its effects on matters other than just legislation are taken into account, such as its (possible) relationship with the cultivation of civic virtue in citizens.[8] Either way, democratic legitimacy is understood with reference to how democracy performs against one or more procedure-independent standards.

Instrumental accounts seem especially vulnerable to reasonable objection. After all, they explicitly rely on procedure-independent standards, and so it is natural to wonder whether said standards are acceptable from all reasonable points of view. In an effort to address this problem, David Estlund argues that an appropriate, relatively uncontroversial standard of assessment is available to instrumentalists. More specifically, he claims that democracy's instrumental value should be assessed in light of whether it is conducive to avoiding what he calls the 'primary bads.' The primary bads include things like genocide, famine, economic collapse, and epidemics. So long as democratic institutions are modestly effective at avoiding them, then democratic legitimacy can appropriately be said to have an instrumental basis, claims Estlund.[9] The reason Estlund thinks that modest instrumental effectiveness suffices is because alternatives that promise equal or greater instrumental value would nonetheless fall prey to reasonable objection. For example, an oligarchic system that places political power in the hands of a benevolent and politically qualified minority might do well at avoiding the primary bads, but it would not be able to supply an acceptable justification for why this minority, and not some other minority, is best qualified to hold power. Any claim that a particular minority group is uniquely qualified to govern is allegedly vulnerable to reasonable objection, and is thus unable to avoid the problem that reasonable disagreement poses for legitimacy.[10]

Estlund's instrumentalism is sophisticated. However, in his efforts to accommodate the problem of reasonable disagreement, he also deprives his theory of its ability to account for democracy's necessary connection with legitimacy. Though he is perhaps right to say that any claim to legitimacy grounded in the alleged political expertise of a particular group is vulnerable to reasonable objection, avoiding the primary bads does not require an oligarchy of the best qualified. As Estlund himself admits in one place, a system that placed voting power in the hands of a randomly selected few might very well possess the same tendency to avoid those bads, so long as forums for public discussion were kept in place to ensure that its heuristic benefits were not lost.[11] Though Estlund seems unperturbed by the possibility that his theory implies an oligarchy drawn by lot may be legitimate, it strikes me as an obvious failing of his account that it has this implication. I take it to be one of our considered judgments—a judgment embedded in our shared political culture—that the denial of universal suffrage deprives a government of legitimacy. The fact that Estlund's theory is inconsistent with this judgment is a serious problem.

A second major approach to understanding democratic justification sees it as a form of pure procedural justice. On this view, legitimacy is not secured via an imperfect tendency to meet some procedure-independent standard, but rather via the intrinsic fairness of democratic procedures. One way of understanding this fairness is with reference to Ronald Dworkin's idea of 'abstract equality.'[12] Thomas Christiano argues that if (a) we take seriously the (allegedly) uncontroversial idea that a legitimate government must equally consider the interests of all citizens, and (b) we take seriously the fact that citizens disagree about which laws and policies should be adopted (perhaps in part because they disagree about some of the requirements of equal consideration), then it follows that democracy is itself a requirement of equal consideration. On the assumption that each citizen has an interest in advancing their own view of what the state should do, equal consideration requires that each citizen be given an equal say over what it does, or so Christiano argues.[13]

Given his reliance on the idea of equal consideration, it might seem peculiar to claim that Christiano's account is non-instrumental. However, any appearance of instrumentalism is superficial. In an instrumental account, it is always possible that some alternative legislative arrangement might satisfy the relevant procedure-independent standard with sufficient reliability and in an acceptable manner. For Christiano's account, however, the above is not true. In his view, having an equal say over what the state does is constitutive of democracy. Furthermore, if we assume the presence of reasonable disagreement, having an equal say is a necessary requirement of equal consideration; it cannot be substituted for some other, equally valid way of achieving abstract equality.

A rather different way of understanding democratic legitimacy can be found in the deliberative democracy tradition, a leading example of which is Joshua Cohen's theory. According to J. Cohen, the relationship between democracy and legitimacy is traceable to the deliberative process that an ideal set of democratic institutions would exhibit. He maintains that insofar as a democracy succeeds in mirroring an ideal deliberative procedure, so too is the enactment of its laws reasonably acceptable to citizens. The conditions of an ideal deliberative procedure include, for example, a requirement that citizens only advance their proposals on the basis of publicly acceptable reasons; a requirement that all citizens formally have equal standing (i.e., an equal vote, the right to put issues on the agenda, and the right to criticize or defend the proposal of others); and a requirement that any inequalities in the distribution of resources not affect citizens' capacity to participate in deliberation.[14]

Overall, the thought that legitimacy is in some way traceable to the intrinsic fairness of democratic procedures is an attractive idea. However, I do not think the above-mentioned accounts successfully cash it out. With respect to J. Cohen's deliberative theory, one issue is that the 'mirroring' relationship between ideal institutions and actual institutions invites dispute. An ideal deliberative procedure is characterized by a mixture of different conditions, and it is difficult to say which should be prioritized in the event that we must choose between them. If, hypothetically speaking, feasible institutional alternative (a) does a better job of encouraging reasoned deliberation, but feasible institutional alternative (b) does a better job of protecting the deliberators' equal standing from the effects of economic inequality, and the set of alternatives that (a) and (b) compose is both exclusive and exhaustive, then which alternative should be chosen? The answer is not obvious, and any answer that might be offered may be vulnerable to reasonable objection.

The deeper problem with J. Cohen's account is that it fundamentally misunderstands legitimacy. Legitimacy is not an aspirational ideal that we presently fall short of and hope one day to eventually achieve. Legitimacy is a virtue that many liberal democracies currently possess. To see whether you agree, consider the implications of claiming that a government is illegitimate. To say that a government is illegitimate is equivalent to saying that it cannot permissibly enforce its laws. What's more, insofar as the authority of a law (the obligation to obey a law because it was enacted) tends not to come apart from its legitimacy, illegitimacy also entails that citizens are not obligated to obey a government's laws. The upshot is that if we were to understand legitimacy the way J. Cohen does, we would in turn be forced to conclude that existing liberal democracies, even those that function comparatively well, cannot justifiably enforce their laws, and that citizens have no obligation to obey the laws. But is this true? Contemporary liberal democracies are certainly far from ideal in many respects. Poverty, discrimination, corruption, and other such problems are present to varying degrees, and reforms that promise to remove or at least reduce these problems ought to be enacted. To say that a society is morally imperfect, however, does not thereby entail that its government is illegitimate, nor does the claim that a government has done less than it could to alleviate social problems. In this sense, legitimacy is unlike many of the values invoked in political debate. Community, distributive fairness, efficiency, and so on are imperfectly realized in any existing democracy. They have been achieved to some extent, but there is still plenty of room for improvement. Legitimacy, by contrast, is a phenomenon to be explained: something we can presently take for granted but should hope to attain a better understanding of. It is not a (possibly unreachable) ideal to strive for.[15]

Christiano's account of democratic legitimacy, by contrast, is close to being on the right track. In particular, I think he is right to claim that democracy is partially constitutive of an important political value, and it is in light of said constitutive relationship that democratic procedures confer legitimacy upon their outputs. However, I think it is a little imprecise to say that democracy is a requirement of equal consideration. The more precise answer is that democracy is a basic requirement of distributive fairness.

In the previous chapter, we concluded that abstract equality is a complex value composed of three value concepts: fairness, concern, and the good. The basic idea was that a government should be concerned for the realization of its citizens' good and that a standard of fairness must constrain the manner in which governments go about facilitating that good. Governments cannot just ignore the good of some citizens and promote the good of others; they must promote citizens' good in a way that is fair.

My criticisms of Christiano should be understood in light of the above understanding of abstract equality. According to the view I favor, democracy is a requirement of one of the values that make up abstract equality—specifically, the fairness part of it. To see why I think so, consider Christiano's view once more. He claims that since citizens disagree over what the state should do, and that since each has an interest in advancing her own political agenda, equal consideration of citizens' interests demands that each be given an equal vote. However, the idea of equal consideration is compatible with other possibilities as well. Suppose it turned out that a plural voting system would advance the interests of the worst-off members of society. It is not implausible to think that giving the better educated members of a society a greater say in politics might have this consequence. Doing so could lead to the adoption of more socially conscious laws and to wiser economic decisions, all of which would advance citizens' interests, the worst-off included. Such policies might even improve the liberty of the worst-off, such as by producing policies that lead to a greater liberty for all or though economic improvements that would enable the worst-off to enjoy the full value of their liberties. What exactly would be wrong with such an arrangement, from the perspective of abstract equality? Abstract equality is interested not only in fairness, but also in the promotion of citizens' interests. By allowing for unequal voting power in the event that it would promote the interests of the worst-off, we strike a balance between the above-mentioned values.

If we think that unequal voting power is illegitimate even when it benefits the worst-off, the reason is because fairness is what connects democracy with legitimacy, not the promotion of interests. What legitimacy requires is a substantively fair, specifically equal distribution of voting power, not a distribution that strikes a balance between fairness and concern.

The following summarizes my position. Like many of the theorists working on democracy, I agree that one of its primary functions is to secure legitimacy by justifying enacted laws to those who may reasonably disagree with them. The question we need to ask is what the content of that justification is. Following theorists such as Christiano and J. Cohen, I agree that democratic procedures are intrinsically fair. Unlike them, however, I think that democracy's procedural fairness should be cashed out with reference to its conformity with a relatively simple, substantive value embedded in our shared political culture, namely, distributive fairness. In my view, democracy and the associated idea of equal voting power are a very basic requirement of distributive fairness. As Christiano correctly notes, the fact of reasonable disagreement over what the state should do suggests that having a say over what the state does is an important social good. If we grant that much, it follows that we have reason to fairly distribute voting power, just as we have reason to fairly distribute income, professional opportunities, and so on. As such, were someone to ask why a procedure that gives everyone an equal vote is the fairest way to address reasonable disagreement, we could justify our choice of procedures by noting that distributive fairness requires it. Since other candidate procedures, such as plural voting or placing voting power in the hands of a randomly selected group, would involve unequal voting power, we can rule them out on the ground that they are sub-optimally fair. A procedure that grants equal voting power to all citizens is part of what constitutes a fair distribution of social goods, and thus it is justified for that reason.

A couple of points about my theory of democratic legitimacy are worth noting. First, substantive fairness's relative simplicity is an important characteristic. It is unlike abstract equality, which is composed of at least a few different moral concepts, and it is unlike the sort of 'justice' that John Rawls is interested in, as his theory adopts principles that reflect a wide variety of normative considerations (e.g., community, fairness, efficiency, stability, publicity, etc.). Substantive fairness, as it is understood here, is a simple value—one of the considerations to be weighed when engaging in practical reasoning about how to design a society's institutions, rather than the output of that reasoning.[16] Because it is simple in this way, it avoids much of the controversy associated with contemporary debates about justice. Questions of justice are controversial, at least in part, because justice theorists are frequently interested in determining how a society's institutions should be designed, all things considered. As such, their theories must, in one way or another, assign weights to all the political values that any plausible theory of this sort must take into account.[17] Unfortunately, the correct assignment of weights is a highly controversial matter. In comparison, then, substantive fairness is an uncontroversial basis upon which to justify democratic procedures. Invoking it in isolation avoids the problem of weightings, and this does a lot to alleviate the worry that our account of democratic justification invites reasonable objection.

Second, insofar as the requirements of fairness are controversial, they are far less controversial when it comes to voting power than when it comes to other things. While we might perhaps reasonably disagree over whether fairness requires an egalitarian distribution of income or whether to include more than just social goods within the metric of fairness, we should nonetheless all be able to agree that fairness requires an equal distribution of voting power. The right to vote is an important liberty, after all, and it is a mainstay of liberal governance that liberties are to be distributed equally. Anyone who thinks otherwise is running afoul of one of the most important judgments located within our shared political culture. Thus, it strikes me as unlikely that any objection to equal liberty would be reasonable.[18]

Third, it is important to my account that substantive fairness is one of the values located within our shared political culture. It is because of its place within this shared culture that considerations of fairness may serve as acceptable reasons in public debate. That substantive fairness is a part of our political culture seems obvious enough. Its frequent appearance in political speeches is a testament to this, as is its frequent appearance in the writing of Western political philosophers. In fact, it seems fair to say that many of the values invoked by politicians and political philosophers are a part of that political culture, such as community, efficiency, publicity, autonomy, and so forth.[19] Unlike other political values, however, fairness has a special role to play in the justification of democratic procedures. After all, the idea that democratic procedures are fair because they satisfy the requirements of distributive fairness is intelligible enough. However, it would be strange to ground the fairness of democratic procedures in other values, such as community or efficiency. The claim that a procedure is fair because it is efficient or that it is fair because it strengthens communal bonds seems conceptually confused.

4. Replies to Criticisms

It might be objected that my dismissal of institutional regulatory principles' claim to primacy is too quick. Though I have argued that no particular set of institutional regulatory principles is necessary or sufficient to secure the legitimacy of law, it is also true that democratically enacted laws must satisfy certain moral requirements in order to be legitimate. It follows that democratic procedure is not sufficient for legitimacy either. The most obvious cases of democratic yet illegitimate laws are those that violate the basic rights and freedoms specified by Rawls's liberty principle. A law that, for example, made it legal to arbitrarily imprison citizens would be illegitimate even if democratically enacted.

My objector is correct to note that the idea of institutional rightness has an important role to play in securing legitimacy. Laws that are patently wrong are also illegitimate, and thus it would not be inappropriate to protest them via acts of civil disobedience. However, I think it is consistent to admit that rightness sets limits on democratic legitimacy while also denying that institutional regulatory principles are appropriately deemed 'the first virtue of institutions.' I will begin by explaining the sense in which rightness limits democratic authority.

It is important to note that no particular conception of institutional rightness limits democratic authority. This follows from the thought that no conception avoids reasonable disagreement. For example, suppose, as I suggested earlier, that there are reasonable alternatives to Rawls's difference principle. In particular, let us suppose that the principle of average utility, when combined with a sufficientarian floor, is such an alternative. If the difference principle is not uniquely reasonable, then proving that some democratically enacted law creates unnecessary inequality would not suffice to delegitimize that law. So long as the law contributes to the maximization of average utility and does not place anyone below the sufficiency threshold, proponents of that conception could reasonably reply that the relevant law is morally fine and that those who disagree should nonetheless respect the authority of democratic procedure. It follows that insofar as there is reasonable disagreement about institutional rightness, a law's failure to conform to a particular conception does not suffice to render it illegitimate.

Though no particular conception avoids reasonable disagreement, there is a degree of overlap between reasonable conceptions. If we can identify commitments that any reasonable conception must share, then we will have succeeded in identifying a set of moral requirements that avoid reasonable disagreement. For example, suppose that the relevant law violated Rawls's liberty principle rather than the difference principle; for example, it legalized arbitrary imprisonment. Such a law is importantly different from one that creates an unnecessary economic inequality because the protection of basic rights and liberties is a relatively uncontroversial matter. Though there is room for disagreement about the scope of certain liberties (freedom of speech, for example) or about the circumstances under which it is appropriate to drop the priority that liberty normally enjoys over other social primary goods, any conception that rejects the importance of protecting basic rights and liberties would be an unreasonable one.[20] As such, the limits upon democratic legitimacy are to be found within the space where reasonable conceptions of institutional morality overlap. If all reasonable conceptions would condemn a particular law, then there can be no reasonable objection to the claim that said law is wrong. And if there is no room for reasonable disagreement about that law's immorality, then democratic justification loses its force.

The limits that institutional rightness sets are important, but it is also important to note that they are, in fact, just limits, and a rather narrow set of limits at that. It is a consequence of reasonable disagreement that institutional rightness radically underdetermines the content of legitimate law. Put another way, answering the question "Which laws would be condemned from all reasonable points of view?" tells us little. It helps us to identify some illegitimate uses of coercion, but it does little to answer the positive question "In what ways may the state legitimately coerce citizens?" By contrast, answering the question "Which laws have been democratically enacted?" is very helpful for discerning legitimate uses of coercion. It is via the act of democratic legislation that a rule becomes an enforceable law in the first place. And if, as I have claimed, democratic procedures express a basic requirement of substantive fairness (the requirement that voting power be distributed equally), then substantive fairness plays a central role in determining the content of legitimate law. Democratically enacted laws are legitimate because they are the output of a procedure that substantive fairness requires us to use.

A second objection one might make against me is that I have misunderstood the concept of legitimacy. I have claimed that legitimacy is a binary concept: a state (as well as a law) either is or is not legitimate; there is no in-between. What's more, I have claimed that legitimacy is something many liberal democracies have already achieved and is thus a phenomenon to be explained rather than an aspirational ideal. Is this really the case, though? Are all legitimate states equally legitimate? My objector might point out that some democracies function much better than others; they make relevant information more accessible to voters, provide more opportunities for public debate, ensure the popular vote is better represented by elected candidates, and so on. If democratic procedure is the primary source of legitimacy, and the degree of fairness that democratic procedures exhibit varies from case to case, then why is legitimacy not a matter of degree too?[21]

The fairness of democratic procedure is certainly a matter of degree, but it is a mistake to think that legitimacy, because it supervenes upon fairness, is therefore also a matter of degree. Threshold concepts sometimes supervene upon concepts that admit of degrees. Consider, for example, membership in the moral community. Moral equality is a binary concept: a being either is or is not the sort of being that possesses universal basic rights (for example, the right to life). However, it is generally thought that whether a being possesses universal basic rights depends on whether she possesses one or more scalar capacities. According to some philosophers, the capacities to feel pain and pleasure and to have a subjective experience of the world are both necessary and sufficient for inclusion in the moral community. Since much animal life is sentient, such philosophers also tend to think that the scope of the moral community extends to animals. According to others, inclusion also requires possessing the rational capacities necessary for praiseworthiness, blameworthiness, and moral responsibility, or in other words, the capacities necessary for moral agency.[22] Either way, it is implausible to think that all beings that possess one or more of the relevant capacities also possess them equally. Different human beings certainly possess rationality to different extents, and the same may very well be true of our capacity for painful or pleasurable experiences (and even if sentience does not vary across humans, it presumably varies across animal species). In spite of this variance, though, moral status is thought to be something that members of the moral community share equally. As such, moral equality is a threshold concept that supervenes upon one or more scalar capacities. So long as a being possesses the relevant capacity or capacities to the necessary minimal extent, it qualifies for membership in the moral community.[23]

Legitimacy should be understood in an analogous manner. Like moral equality, it supervenes upon a scalar property, namely the fairness of democratic procedures. As I have already argued, that citizens have an equal say over the use of state power is a requirement of substantive fairness. And since having an equal say is constitutive of democracy: democracy is itself a requirement of substantive fairness. But actually securing an equal say requires more than just protecting a formal right to vote. It requires ensuring many things, such as that citizens have equal access to the information needed to form an educated political opinion, that they have an equal opportunity to voice their opinions in public forums, and so on. However, so long as a democratic government has secured an equal say to the necessary minimum extent, I think it is best to think of it as legitimate. Correctly specifying that minimum is tricky, but it is clear that full legitimacy obtains once some sort of threshold is met. The alternative would be to conclude that the justifiability of enforcement is, like fairness, a scalar property, that is, that it is only a little bit justifiable for certain liberal democracies to enforce their laws, but very justifiable for other liberal democracies to enforce their laws. Better to instead say that some governments are simply unjustified in using coercion (tyrannies, for example) whereas other are justified (most liberal democracies), but that some of those which are justified are nonetheless imperfectly fair.

5. Conclusion

In conclusion, I have argued that democratic legitimacy is grounded in democracy's relationship with distributive fairness. More specifically, I have argued that making political decisions via a procedure that grants all citizens an equal say over the use of state power is a basic, uncontroversial requirement of distributive fairness, and that distributive fairness is thus an appropriate basis upon which to understand democracy's ability to resolve the problem of reasonable disagreement. This conclusion has important implications for the main thesis of my book, that is, my claim that the pluralist understanding of justice's narrowness is correct. As we have noted, the pervasiveness of reasonable disagreement makes democracy more important to legitimacy than institutional rightness. Furthermore, the fairness of democratic procedure is itself traceable to the idea that substantive fairness requires securing an equal say for citizens (or an equal distribution of voting power, as I sometimes put it). The upshot, it would seem, is that substantive fairness, despite being a defeasible value, has a better claim to primacy than institutional regulatory principles do. Assuming that primacy is an important part of the concept of narrow justice, substantive fairness therefore also has a better claim to the title of 'justice.'

Notes

1. See, for example, Arneson (1993) pp. 118–48; Christiano (2008); Estlund (2008); and Cohen (2002).
2. See John Rawls's thoughts about reasonable pluralism in Rawls (1993) pp. 36–7, as well his thoughts about legitimacy in Rawls (1993) pp. 136–7.
3. Rawls (2001) pp. 139–40.
4. Rawls (2001) pp. 138–9.
5. See Cohen (2009); and Arneson (2015) pp. 222–5.
6. Arneson (1993); and Estlund (2008). For a discussion of the idea of imperfect procedural justice, see Rawls (1971) pp. 85–6.
7. Christiano (2008); and J. Cohen (2002). For a discussion of the idea of pure procedural justice, see Rawls (1971) p. 86.
8. For the above distinction between kinds of instrumentalism, see Arneson (2003) p. 123.
9. Estlund (2008) pp. 160–7.
10. Estlund (2008) pp. 33–6 and pp. 211–8.
11. Estlund (2008) pp. 181–2.
12. Dworkin (2000) pp. 1–3.
13. See Christiano (2002); and Christiano (2008) Chapter 3.
14. J. Cohen (2002) pp. 91–4.
15. For further discussion of the idea that legitimacy is a binary concept, see the second half of section 4 in the present chapter.

16. See G. A. Cohen's discussion of fairness in Cohen (2008) pp. 6–8. For similar discussions, see Segall (2007) pp. 188–91, Swift (2008) pp. 382–7; and Tomlin (2010) pp. 240–6.
17. See Rawls's discussion of weighing values in Rawls (1971) pp. 34–45.
18. Rawls notes, and I agree, that a view that rejects the essentials of a "democratic regime" is unreasonable. I also presume that equal voting power is such an essential. See Rawls (1993) p. xvi and pp. 61–2.
19. For a helpful discussion of the political values embedded in our shared political culture, see Rawls (1999) pp. 146–7.
20. Protecting basic rights and liberties is one of the essentials of a democratic regime. See footnote 18 in the present chapter.
21. I owe thanks to Jeremy Butler and Alex Wellington for raising this problem with me.
22. For different views about the capacities necessary and sufficient for moral status, and about the scope of moral equality, see, for example, Singer (1975); and Cohen and Regan (2001).
23. For further discussion of the idea that moral equality, though a binary concept, supervenes upon scalar capacities, see Carter (2011).

References

Arneson, Richard. 1993. "Democratic Rights at Rational and Workplace Levels." In *The Ideal of Democracy*. Eds. David Copp, Jean Hampton, and John F. Roemer (Cambridge: Cambridge University Press). Pp. 118–48.

Arneson, Richard. 2003. "Defending the Purely Instrumental Account." *The Journal of Political Philosophy* 11: 122–32.

Arneson, Richard. 2015. "Why Not Capitalism?" In *Distributive Justice and Access to Advantage*. Ed. Alexander Kaufman (Cambridge: Cambridge University Press). Pp. 207–34.

Carter, Ian. 2011. "Respect and the Basis of Equality." *Ethics* 121: 538–71.

Christiano, Thomas. 2002. "Democracy as Equality." In *Democracy*. Ed. David Estlund (Malden, MA: Blackwell Publishing). Pp. 31–50.

Christiano, Thomas. 2008. *The Constitution of Equality* (New York: Oxford University Press).

Cohen, Carl and Tom Regan. 2001. *The Animal Rights Debate* (Lanham: Rowman & Littlefield).

Cohen, G.A. 2008. *Rescuing Justice and Equality* (Cambridge, MA: Harvard University Press).

Cohen, G.A. 2009. *Why Not Socialism?* (Princeton: Princeton University Press).

Cohen, Joshua. 2002. "Deliberation and Democratic Legitimacy." In *Democracy*. Ed. David Estlund (Malden, MA: Blackwell Publishing). Pp. 87–106.

Dworkin, Ronald. 2000. *Sovereign Virtue: The Theory and Practice of Equality* (Cambridge, MA: Harvard University Press).

Estlund, David. 2008. *Democratic Authority: A Philosophical Framework* (Princeton: Princeton University Press).

Rawls, John. 1971. *A Theory of Justice* (Cambridge, MA: Belknap Press).

Rawls, John. 1993. *Political Liberalism* (New York: Columbia University Press).

Rawls, John. 1999. *The Law of Peoples with "The Idea of Public Reason Revisited."* (Cambridge, MA: Harvard University Press).

Rawls, John. 2001. *Justice as Fairness: A Restatement*. Ed. Erin Kelly (Cambridge, MA: Belknap Press).

Segall, Shlomi. 2007. "In Solidarity with the Imprudent: A Defense of Luck Egalitarianism." *Social Theory and Practice* 33: 177–98.

Singer, Peter. 1975. *Animal Liberation* (New York: Avon Books).

Swift, Adam. 2008. "The Value of Philosophy in Non-Ideal Circumstances." *Social Theory and Practice* 34: 363–87.

Tomlin, Patrick. 2010. "Survey Article: Internal Doubts about Cohen's Rescue of Justice." *The Journal of Political Philosophy* 18: 228–47.

7 Conclusion

1. Summary

My book has focused on two competing ways of understanding the Aristotelian claim that 'justice,' though sometimes used to refer to moral rightness in general, also has a narrower sense that refers to a part of moral rightness. The first way understands narrowness to be a matter of context specificity. On this view, narrow justice is about the moral rightness of specifically institutions. The second understanding, in contrast, sees narrowness as a matter of singularity against a plural background. On this view, narrow justice is one among a plurality of fundamental values.

My overarching purpose has been to establish the plausibility and theoretical significance of a pluralist understanding of narrowness. To establish theoretical significance in particular, I connected the pluralist understanding of narrowness to two major debates between contemporary egalitarian political philosophers: the debate over luck egalitarianism and the debate over justice's scope of application. In Chapter 3, I argued that the harshness objection, Samuel Scheffler's concerns about free will, and Jonathan Wolff's worries about respect are critically effective against luck egalitarianism as a theory of all-things-considered institutional rightness. When luck egalitarianism is understood as a conception of a fundamental value, however, these problems merely limit the extent to which luck equality should be implemented via derivative regulatory principles.

With respect to justice's scope of application, I argued in Chapter 4 that G. A. Cohen frequently equivocates when responding to the demandingness problem and to criticisms related to the causal relationship between a society's institutions and ethos. Though many of his replies make sense if one is defending the application of a fundamental value to personal choice, such as his personal prerogative qualification and the inclusion of subjective welfare in one's metric, they become problematic when it is acknowledged that the issue at hand is whether the difference principle (an institutional regulatory principle) extends to personal choice. I concluded that a regulatory alternative modeled on Peter Singer's public standard of assistance would be both a better guide to action and substantively fairer than a welfare-inclusive, prerogative-constrained difference principle.

To establish the plausibility of pluralist narrowness, I argued in Chapter 5 that the Rawlsian case for replacing a substantive understanding of fairness with a procedural one is ill-advised. I claimed that the legitimacy-related worry about arbitrarily adopting regulatory principles, when applied to the selection of procedural devices, requires us to employ substantive fairness at the procedural level. Without a substantive principle of fairness, we cannot justify the claim that our procedural device is itself fair and thus cannot resolve the problem that arbitrariness poses for the justified exercise of state coercion. The upshot of this reliance upon substantive fairness is that justified regulatory principles are non-identical with justice itself. If we want to know what justice itself is, we need to theorize the fundamental value from which both contractualist procedures and institutional regulatory principles ultimately derive their fairness. And as I argued in Chapter 3, luck egalitarianism is the best theory of that value.

To complete my case for the plausibility of pluralist narrowness, Chapter 6 argues that democracy is best understood as a basic requirement of substantive fairness, namely, the requirement that citizens be given an equal say over the exercise of state power. If substantive fairness grounds democracy, then it is also of central importance to the legitimate exercise of coercion, which in turn suggests that it has a claim to primacy in the institutional context. It seems that considerations of not only fairness, but also primacy, favor the pluralist interpretation of narrowness.

In the remainder of this chapter, I will draw attention to some of the implications of my work, as well as to areas where future research would be productive. Of particular interest is the significance of my work for the methodology of political philosophy.

2. Methodological Implications

In Chapter 2, I drew a picture of what is involved in giving a conception of a fundamental value. As was discussed, the process is similar but not identical to reflective equilibrium. Whereas the goal of reflective equilibrium, as it is normally understood, is to achieve coherence between a set of action-guiding principles and our (hopefully) shared pool of all-things-considered intuitive judgments, the process via which a conception of a fundamental value is justified requires reference specifically to judgments belonging to that value. The normative force these judgments possess is oft times of the defeasible, ceteris paribus kind, and identifying them requires drawing a boundary between intuitive judgments internal to the value under analysis and those external to it. When justifying a conception of personal autonomy, for example, the goal is to achieve coherence with judgments that bear upon the autonomy of actions and that, if neglected, would challenge our conception's adequacy as a criterion that supplies conditions necessary and sufficient for an action to count as autonomous, for example, the judgment that actions one was brainwashed to perform are heteronymous.

The sort of boundary drawing needed to theorize fundamental values can be performed in a rough and ready way. So long as the theorist has a rough understanding of the value concept she is trying to form a conception of, she should be able to tell which intuitive judgments are relevant and which ones bear upon other values. However, it is always possible for a dispute to emerge over whether or not a judgment is internal. The reason such dispute is possible is because we do not always have a perfectly adequate, pre-theoretical understanding of the value concepts we employ, and because the words we employ to refer to fundamental values sometimes refer to other concepts with which the value under analysis may be confused. For example, as we noted in Chapter 2, the word 'efficient' is frequently used in everyday language to refer to cases where an agent effectively and economically pursues whatever her goal or goals may be. Understood this way, the importance of efficiency is always parasitic upon whatever the relevant goal is, and in cases where the goal is harmful or otherwise bad, so is efficiency. There is, however, another sense of the word frequently employed by economists, philosophers, and decision theorists in discussions of Pareto-optimality and utility maximization.[1] This quantitative sense of 'efficiency' is less flexible than the everyday sense, as it is only predicable of things that we can intelligibly apply 'amount' language to (e.g., aggregate amount, total amount, etc.), and it is always restricted to what might be termed 'metric concepts'. (e.g., resources, subjective welfare, flourishing, etc.). It is also the sense intended by those (such as myself) who understand efficiency to be a value.

When a dispute over the internality of a judgment emerges either due to an imperfect understanding of a value concept or due to confusion over a term's referent, there is only one way to resolve it: conceptual analysis. Since the publication of Rawls's *Theory of Justice*, conceptual analysis has lost much of the interest it once had for political philosophers. They have turned their gaze from what some think of as semantic quibbles towards substantive normative debate. If the approach to theorizing fundamental values I have laid out is correct, though, then conceptual analysis has an important place in value theory. It is through conceptual analysis that a rough understanding of a value concept becomes more refined. Thus it is a tool that can be used to draw the boundary between judgments internal and external to a value with as much precision as possible. What's more, conceptual analysis can shed light on cases where disputants do not realize that they are using the same word to refer to two different things and can thus help them to avoid talking past each other. Once disputants are aware that they are using the same term to refer to different concepts, they can then have a productive discussion about which concept is a fundamental value and thus worthy of being theorized. With respect to efficiency, in particular, the answer was easy. The everyday use of the term, because it is both instrumental and flexible enough to attach to bad goals, cannot plausibly be thought of as a value. As a result, only the quantitative sense of the term is a plausible candidate. In other cases, however, the answer is less clear. The word 'freedom,' for example, is a rather messy one. It (ostensibly) has a negative sense, a positive sense, a metaphysical sense, and a 'political' sense explicated in Rawls's later work.[2] Given that many of these can plausibly be thought of as having significance for normative theory, the question "Which concept of freedom, if any, is a fundamental value?" is not a foolish one to ask.

With respect to further work in the area, it strikes me that it would be worthwhile to survey what literature there is on the many value concepts employed in normative political philosophy in order to determine the degree to which they have or have not been adequately theorized to date. How many conceptions of community are out there? Of compassion? Of respect? As frequently as value concepts like these are appealed to in political argument, it is far rarer for the philosophers who use them to attempt to justify, or even to specify, their particular conceptions of them in advance of their use. Even when theorists do specify and attempt to justify conceptions of the fundamental values they employ, their justifications might not be sufficiently attentive to the need to draw a boundary between judgments that are relevant to those values and judgments that are not relevant. Undertaking a survey of all the theoretical literature concerning fundamental values would obviously be a mammoth task, but it is also a necessary one if we hope to get a better sense of the precise content of all our different fundamental values, not just substantive fairness.

Though I have devoted considerable space to justifying a particular conception of substantive fairness (I argued that substantive fairness is luck equality), I have not comprehensively specified its content. In particular, one matter I left unaddressed is the metric of substantive fairness. Since there is a huge literature on questions of metric, I will not argue here for a particular answer to this question. I mainly want to note that this is yet another area where more work could productively be done. I will say, however, that the proposition that a distributive metric should include subjective welfare is more plausible at the level of fundamental values than it is at the level of distributive regulatory principles. As we noted in Chapter 4 during our discussion of demandingness and compensation for special labor burdens, including subjective welfare in the metric of distributive regulatory principles compromises their capacity for action guidance, as measurability issues make it difficult to interpersonally compare subjective welfare levels. Substantive fairness, in contrast, is a fundamental value, and thus empirical facts about measurability do not affect its content. If, as G. A. Cohen suggests, we share an intuitive judgment to the effect that unchosen welfare deficiencies are unfair (such as the deficiency experienced by a wheelchair-occupying individual unable to raise his arms without experience pain), then we have good reason to seek coherence with that judgment by including subjective welfare in the metric of luck equality.[3] The regulatory implications of including subjective welfare at the fundamental level would require some work to determine. It is likely that there would be implications of some sort, though. For example, it may become especially important to pursue an egalitarian distribution of whatever material goods strongly affect opportunities for welfare.

Shifting now to the level of regulatory theory, one notable implication is that the justification of a set of regulatory principles is sometimes temporary.

If, for example, a fact responsible for putting two values in conflict with each other ceases to hold true at some point down the road, either due to chance or to our own efforts, then regulatory principles that owe their plausibility in part to their responsiveness to that conflict should now be revised. With the conflict having dissolved, we can now hope to implement the values that matter to us to a greater extent, and the content of our regulatory principles should change to reflect this. It was for this reason that I recommended amending the difference principle once inequalities between social groups have been sufficiently reduced. Without significant social inequalities, Jonathan Wolff's concern about an unequal distribution of scrutiny and the resulting expression of disrespect towards disadvantaged social groups would no longer be operative. The amendment I suggested making once such a state of affairs has been achieved is that the difference principle specifically maximize the position of those who are less well-off through no fault of their own, and that a sufficientarian standard be used to safeguard the basic needs of the imprudent. Such a principle would implement a greater degree of substantive fairness without sacrificing other values of interest.

Notes

1. See Macleod (1998).
2. See Berlin (2002); and Rawls (1985).
3. Cohen (1989) pp. 917–9.

References

Berlin, Isaiah. 2002. "Two Concepts of Liberty." In *Liberty: Incorporating Four Essays on Liberty*. Ed. Henry Hardy (Oxford: Oxford University Press).

Cohen, G.A. 1989. "On the Currency of Egalitarian Justice." *Ethics* 99: 906–44.

Macleod, Alistair. 1998. "Efficiency and Justice." In "Law, Justice & Culture." *Arsp-Beiheft*. Vol. 68. Eds. Andre-Jean Arnaud & Peter Koller (Stuttgart: Franz Steiner). Pp. 111–9.

Rawls, John. 1985. "Justice as Fairness: Political Not Metaphysical." *Philosophy and Public Affairs* 14: 223–51.

Index

For Product Safety Concerns and Information please contact our EU
representative GPSR@taylorandfrancis.com
Taylor & Francis Verlag GmbH, Kaufingerstraße 24, 80331 München, Germany

www.ingramcontent.com/pod-product-compliance
Ingram Content Group UK Ltd.
Pitfield, Milton Keynes, MK11 3LW, UK
UKHW021958180926
475701UK00003B/81

* 9 7 8 0 3 6 7 3 7 2 0 6 4 *